Big Tales
from My
Little Farm

by

Farmer Chris

with Chris Berry

Foreword by

Julian Norton

GREAT NORTHERN

Great Northern Books
PO Box 1380, Bradford,
West Yorkshire, BD5 5FB

www.greatnorthernbooks.co.uk

ISBN: 978-1-914227-30-1

Design by David Burrill

CIP Data
A catalogue for this book is available
from the British Library

To Kate

I could never have done any of this without you.
I love you for everything you are, everything you do
and for simply being you.

Love you always, Chris
(or should that be Oh Christopher!) x

To Mum & Dad

To the best parents I could ever have wished for. Thank
you for your unconditional and unstinting love and
support.
Mum, like you I miss Dad every day, but I know he will
be looking down on us with a smile and probably a
laugh or two at my efforts!

Love you both, Chris x

FOREWORD

Julian Norton

"I'm really worried, Julian," was the first thing that Chris said on the phone. "The thing is, she's my favourite cow."

I'd heard similar things from Chris many times before. Not that he was a panicking farmer. Far from it. Chris was usually very level-headed and calm. It just seemed that every time something went slightly wrong with any of his animals, it always seemed to be his favourite; or his best; or his rarest; or his cutest; or his best mate.

On this occasion, it was a cow called Bertha. Her eye was not right. Could I call and visit? Of course I could. Maybe tomorrow evening, after I'd finished evening surgery? Bertha's problem would not be so easy to resolve, but more of that later.

If it wasn't Bertha, it was Lucky the piglet, stuck beyond arm's length in a favourite Oxford Sandy and Black sow (aka a Plum Pudding Pig, as Chris always reiterated).

I rushed out, as soon as I could relieve myself from other, pre-organised, work and assisted in a rare and unusual farrowing. Most vets don't get to do this so often these days, so it was a joy to assist. Or it could just as easily have been one of his terriers, having recently delivered a litter of pups without need of special veterinary attention. A health check for the whole litter was *de rigueur*.

One thing is for sure. All the animals at Spring View Farm are equally loved and respected. Pigs, sheep, dogs, horses, but especially the herd which consists of the famous Whitebred Shorthorn. They are (according to Chris, and I hear this every time) rarer than the Giant Panda. And I thought they were rare because their diet consisted exclusively of white bread! I was wrong on this one.

But what I've learnt from my workings and time with Chris is this. It isn't about the breed of cattle, or the unusual type of sheep or pig. What makes farmers fun to work with is the enthusiasm they have for their lifestyle and the animals with which they co-habit and work. Passion and enthusiasm is key. It motivates everyone around – whether a veterinary surgeon or a producer-director off the telly. Fortunately, Chris has enthusiasm in abundance. And this is evident in every paragraph of this wholesome book. I hope you enjoy it.

Julian Norton

INTRODUCTION

Thank you for buying this, my second book. I can hardly believe I'm saying that, as I'd never thought I would have ever written one, let alone two.

If you bought *Farming, Celebs & Plum Pudding Pigs – The Making of Farmer Chris* and you're back for a second helping of my life, I'm really honoured and truly thrilled that you consider it worthwhile enough to spend several hours of your life with me reading about what I have done.

This time *Big Tales from My Little Farm* is about the trials and tribulations, the agony and ecstasy that my lovely wife Kate and I have gone through ever since we took on our little corner of paradise in North Yorkshire. It has been messy, it has been wonderful, it has been crazy, it has been emotional. I've been an idiot, I've been inspired, I've been at the lowest of lows and the highest of highs and I wouldn't trade any of it for the world.

Those of you who remember the stories in the first book won't be surprised to read that my life has been and continues to be one of significant ups and downs, highs and lows, some of them brought on by myself – well, at least the lows and the bits where I've got things catastrophically wrong have been down to me. The highs? Well, maybe they come more from good fortune and working hard.

Having my own farm was all I really ever wanted and it has brought me so much happiness and fulfilment. There is nothing that beats seeing a new calf, new lamb or new piglet being born and as I write we are currently in the midst of much new life arriving on our little farm this year.

I have been very lucky to have enjoyed my own small modicum of fame through my TV appearances on *The Yorkshire Vet* and *Celebs on the Farm*, but it is my farm, my wife and my animals that mean more to me than anything.

I shall also be forever grateful that my publishers Great Northern Books have shown such confidence in publishing both of my books. I would like to personally thank David Burrill at GNB and my good friend and author Chris Berry, once again, for putting my words into the right order and expressing what I truly feel.

I hope you have a few laughs along the way. I'm embarrassed about some things, I often wonder about my own sanity and Kate regularly despairs with me I know, but I am who I am, I'm Farmer Chris. I'm a farmer, I have my own farm and there are some big tales to tell. Welcome to *Big Tales from My Little Farm*!

CONTENTS

CHAPTER 1

FARMER

Never Any Doubt

I never had any doubt in my mind that I was meant to be a farmer. It has always been in my head, my heart, my soul, even if I didn't have my own farm until seven and a half years ago when Kate and I moved into Spring View Farm in the hamlet of Thornton on the Hill. It was always there within me.

My dad worked on farms and had a 20-acre smallholding at Scriven House Farm in Wigginton near York where he had cows and pigs. My granddad had had a 50-acre farm at Oak Lea Farm in the village that he worked with horses and I always believed that somehow, someway, I would follow them and have my own farm with cattle, sheep and pigs.

Farming is in my DNA. It is in my blood. I feel it very strongly, but it wasn't until we arrived here at Spring View that my dream was finally brought to reality.

Seven and a half years! Good Grief! How time flies. We've done so much, been through so much and of course now, thanks to my appearances on television, I'm not even just a farmer but now known by some as Farmer Chris.

I like it that people know me this way. It's a really nice feeling, but I have many who also now know me through the farm itself, through our pedigree rare breed animals or through the business Kate and I run together called Green's Country Store in Thirsk Livestock Market.

I recognised right from the start of becoming Farmer Chris, when we filmed the first *Celebs on the Farm* series, that being associated with a nationally viewed television programme brought with it an additional

responsibility because of my role in the show and how farming would come across.

All of a sudden, I would be seen as a farmer and I was determined to represent farmers and farming in the best way possible. I hope, if you watched my efforts, that you feel I did just that.

When you read some of what has happened in these *Big Tales from My Little Farm* you might question my judgment at times, my sanity and my farming ability. I know I certainly do in those darker moments, but I'm telling you these tales because some are funny, some are very sad, some are ridiculous, some serious, others joyous, soul searching, incredible, regretful, idiotic and chaotic. Some are all of these. And I know many will resonate with other farmers, no matter how much some may not want to say.

Right, I'm going to hide behind the sofa now or go for a long walk around the farm while you read each story. Feel free to dip in and out of this book wherever you choose. You can read each one as a separate story.

CHAPTER 2

SHEEP

I Thought You Liked Lambing

This next line is quite true. Livestock had started arriving at Spring View Farm before we started living here.

Literally the minute I had walked through the farmhouse door, when we viewed the farm, I knew that I wanted to buy this place. It was a bit rough, untidy and decidedly smelly, but it was just like somebody had jumped inside me and had said, 'Get this place'. It's perfect.

It was only a 10-acre farm, no more than a smallholding to many farmers, but I was like a kid in a sweetshop. I just thought, Wow! I can really do something with this.

I was immediately thinking how many pigs I could get, how many sheep, how many cattle I could run, how many calves I could rear. Everything was going through my head. This is all very possible. I want to be here.

Kate is a farmer's daughter. We are both from farming families. She used to show sheep all around Yorkshire and at the Great Yorkshire Show. Perfect. Perfect. Perfect. We bought it. More of that later.

I just had to have stock on the farm as soon as I could, so off I went to Britain's Sexiest Sheep Farmer, as you do!

Now just in case you're thinking this book is going the same way as some of my earlier exploits in the first book, think again.

The young lady is Anna Simpson of Windy Hill Farm, Hutton Rudby and used to work with Kate and I. Anna had won the title through a *Farmer's Weekly* competition in 2010 and was one of our sales advisers.

Anna was going out of sheep at the time and I bought 50 Mule ewes and borrowed a Texel tup from another young lady who worked for us and had sheep, Hayley Wood.

To the uninitiated the North of England Mule is a crossbreed of a Swaledale ewe that is put to a Bluefaced Leicester tup; and Texels originated in Holland from the Isle of Texel. The breed is one of the most popular rams used to create lambs that will be sold for meat.

It wasn't as though I'd had any grand idea at the time about what kind of sheep I wanted. I just wanted to have some sheep and thought let's get them.

It was such a lovely thing. These were the first animals on Spring View Farm. Arriving before us! We had stock! I'm a proper farmer at last and even though I'm not there yet, they are!

So, if we're keeping score, that gave me 50 animals on the farm before we even owned it!

You see even before Day 1 of moving in and way before I became known as Farmer Chris, I already had my eyes firmly fixed on filling up the farm with stock. I remember thinking, I don't just want an empty house, empty buildings and empty fields! I want some stock running about.

At this point I must tell you that the most common theme you will read in this book is, 'I'd not thought it through, had I?'

Poor Kate hadn't quite realised what I would be doing and pointed out, through her own very straightforward and common-sense manner, delivered as always with the variable degrees of patience, love, despair and sometimes a little disdain: "You do realise, Christopher, that in buying 50 Mules and a Texel tup that sometime in April we are going to be lambing them."

There may also have been a mention of how this could be achieved while running our business, trying to turn our new home habitable. I probably chose to ignore this.

Instead, I said: "I thought you liked lambing!"

You can probably imagine the look I received, but with hands like I have I'm not the one who can get those lambs out when help is needed. But Kate can!

And I knew I would need my better half's, as always, amazing support in order for my purchase of 50 ewes to expand our numbers to 125 in a matter of months when lambing time came around!

I knew that my reasoning for getting sheep had been based on sound sheep farming practice even though it may have looked like I'd not thought this through.

But I really had!

We were to move in on 2 November 2015 and if you want to have lambs on the ground in April you need to have your ewes tupped from the first week in November. We had to get a wriggle on as it was bang on the time the tup needed to be going in with ewes.

But there's a lot more to sheep than just lambing. I'd not thought it through at all, as it turned out.

CHAPTER 3

SHEEP

I'd Have Been Thrown Off
Celebs on the Farm

We have a hill behind the farmhouse and it's where the farm gets its name from as there is such a lovely view from it. We are about 400 feet above sea level at this point and while that's nothing like being a Dales or moors farmer at 1000 feet and more, it does make you feel as though you're a hill farmer when you're stood there with your crook and sheep all around you.

It felt fantastic to me, very special, and it always will.

But it's one thing looking the part and another thing knowing what you're doing!

Our first problem, way in advance of lambing, was gathering the sheep. You need to do this to undertake jobs like vaccinations, worming, treatments for such as flystrike and simply to check them over.

They all needed their annual vaccine. We had to catch them and once we'd done that we had to turn them on to their bottoms so we could take a look at their feet, trim them and spray with antibiotic spray.

I hadn't realised the enormity of being able to take on these tasks and it took us longer to gather them up than it took to treat them.

I had worked with sheep before, but I'd never owned any and suddenly you are responsible for the welfare of these animals. It's called animal husbandry. You have a duty of care to every animal and having your own animals brings that home to you. Anything you have to do with them means catching and holding them.

And if you can't round them up, you can't check them over. And if you haven't a sheepdog it really is hard work. And even if I'd had a sheepdog I'd have had to train it up. And I would need training in doing that even before I got a sheepdog.

Had I thought this through?

No, I had not. Did we have a sheepdog? No. We have Jack Russell terriers and they are certainly not suitable for the task.

Did we have a quad bike? That's what other sheep farmers have. Nope.

Oh my God, we had nothing. Add to this that Kate can't run and I can only run a little better and we just can't catch the bloody things!

So, there was I, shouting at Kate to go one way and then the other, both with our arms outstretched. She's waving a bit of blue pipe around, why the hell I don't know because it's bloody useless. I'm now shouting at her and the sheep. One lot are going in one direction, another lot are going another way and there's even a third lot going in another direction. I thought sheep were all supposed to follow each other? Not ours, obviously.

What an absolute disaster! If I'd been one of the celebrities off my own television show I'd have given myself a right rollicking and at the end of the day in the barn when I would normally make a decision as to which one should go, I would have thrown myself off right there and then! Caprice would have been wailing with laughter. It was laughable. But not at the time!

But we learned. Fortunately, we have been in the business of supplying all kinds of goods to farmers for many years and we had sheep handling equipment at our base at Thirsk. We bought some of the kit and made ourselves a basic penning system and race out of rails and gates. It means you can funnel the sheep into you, one by one, once you've collected them in.

At first our saviour was a bucket. A yellow bucket. Sheep love food. Maybe they think it's a welcome change from grass, I don't know, but they love food and they soon realised that if I came out with this yellow bucket it meant there was something for them. That's how I got them to follow me so that we could get them rounded up.

It worked for a while but you can't keep feeding sheep additional feed to the grass they eat because if the ewes keep eating then the lambs inside them can get too big that it makes lambing the ewes a nightmare. And we already had enough nightmares to come without adding another!

Anyone who has ever had sheep will also tell you that they appear to have only one ambition – and that is to die. You can do everything right with them, look after them like they are your prized possessions, you can bend over backwards, you can keep giving them every medicine in the world to keep them alive and you can still go out the next morning and the inevitable has happened.

We were extremely fortunate in our first winter. It was quite a wet winter but not particularly harsh. I tended to them every day and we didn't have a single ewe die on us and apart from the initial disaster with rounding them up, or in our case not being able to, everything seemed to go reasonably well in that way, although we did have quite a few go lame, which we brought in and treated.

Sheep just seem to decide they are going to go lame no matter what you've tried to do to help them.

Another thing we hadn't thought through, or to be perfectly accurate I hadn't thought through, was fencing.

Our land was reasonably fenced, but not greatly fenced. Sheep don't understand the difference between reasonably or greatly. All they understand is an escape route. Their second favourite occupation after finding new ways to expire is apparently to perform a quick exit.

Not only were we not able to round up our sheep, they were also now introducing themselves to our neighbours' rhododendrons in the next village! We had one or two reports of their wanderings which led me to decide, pretty quickly, that I had to make the farm neither reasonably or greatly fenced, but wholly fenced.

I set about the task and managed to get every boundary fenced or re-fenced that winter.

A quicker solution would probably have been to get a sheepdog, but sheepdogs need to work and we weren't really big enough to keep one busy, not with just 50 sheep. And since I'd never worked sheepdogs it would probably also have been another case of, guess what, having not thought it through. You're getting the idea.

CHAPTER 4

DOGS

Timmy & the Chocolate Orange

We might not have a sheepdog, but we do have dogs. Four of them, all Jack Russell terriers. There's Poppy. She's the old girl, about 14 years old. She's quiet and calm, or at least she is in comparison to the rest. She came from a puppy farm!

I had seen an advertisement for a Jack Russell for sale in a local newspaper. I'd just thought it was going to be someone who couldn't cope with having a dog any longer for whatever the reason.

When I reached the house in Marske by the Sea I was shocked to see all these puppies in a garden shed of a house on a housing estate.

I couldn't believe it! A puppy farm! I just knew there and then that I had to save her. She was just six weeks old. It was all quite sad seeing all of those other puppies and I wished I could have taken more because I just felt it wasn't right.

Poppy is Kate's dog. She replaced Tillie who Kate had before her. Poppy loves watching television and one thing she always does that amazes me is that she barks when she sees a dog on screen. How does a dog differentiate? How does she know? Clearly she does.

We love going to the isle of Barra in the Outer Hebrides and usually take all the dogs, but as I said Poppy is now getting on a bit and won't be going with us in future as she has a touch of arthritis. The other three will all be coming. They love it as much as we do.

Kate and I have had Jack Russells for years. It was Kate who got me started with them and I wouldn't be without them come what may.

Someone once said the worst part about keeping a dog is the day it goes, whether it dies naturally, or for one reason or another it has to be put down to save it from suffering. Whoever said it was spot on. It really is so true.

It was brought home to me in wave after wave of emotion when I lost Pip, my dog before I got Peggy.

Pip was the dog Kate bought me before we lived together. Company for me, is how Kate had explained. We were both living separately at the time. I'd moved into this house in Easingwold, and Kate had said I needed a dog. I couldn't believe how right she had been because I loved her so much.

Pip and I went everywhere together, just like Peggy and I do today, and I was broken-hearted when she went. I still have a picture of her at the farm.

Every night, for months after Pip had gone, I would go to that picture on my chest of drawers and I would kiss it. Kissing her, my little dog, my little friend who I'd loved so much and shared so much.

There you go. That's Farmer Chris, the great soft thing I really am, not this grumpy sod going around like a bear with a sore head when things go wrong. I know that when any of our dogs go that I'll feel similarly. Not the same, that much I know, because obviously Pip was very, very special to me and God knows what I'll be like when Peggy goes!

Anyhow, I was telling you about Poppy and now I've mentioned Peggy. There's also Lottie and our bundle of trouble, Timmy.

The thing about all four of them and all Jack Russells

is that rather like people they all have their own character, they are all very different.

Lottie is so inquisitive. She's always looking to see what's going on, very nosey. And we do have an issue with Peggy and Lottie. I don't know why it is, but they just don't get on sometimes. It's particularly evident when someone comes to the door. It must be some kind of competitive instinct they have for being top dog because they will both go straight for the door, barking at it, and within a second they can turn on each other. It's not all the time, but it's quite alarming when it happens.

You would think it was a real dog fight. You can see their teeth bared and they are obviously angry with each other. They do make contact as well, there's nothing held back. I won't go into further detail here other than to mention jowls and ears! Because of this tendency we have to manage them closely and it appears as though it may have calmed down as, touch wood, we haven't experienced that kind of mayhem in a while.

Ratting is their speciality. We never had them to do a specific job but they all really come into their own when it comes to ratting! We don't get too many rats, but crikey if there's a rat about then our pack of Jack Russells know how to sort it out. I don't think they knowingly work as a pack but they are very successful. They might not be any good for rounding up sheep but getting rid of vermin is where they come into their own.

Because Kate and I have a business to run and dogs need exercise we used to take our dogs to work. That was when we just had the two – Pip and Tillie – but you can't take four of them. It would be carnage in the office and unfair on the rest of the team, so we leave them at home as our mini guard-dog troop on the farm. They get plenty of exercise because our garden is a reasonable size. We will hopefully walk them more than we do currently in the near future if all goes according to plan.

More of what we are planning in another of these tales.

Peggy is my girl. I still call her my puppy even though as I write she's now 9 years old. She's the one you will see on the television with me whether on *The Yorkshire Vet* or *Celebs on the Farm.*

I've never had a dog so committed to me, not even Pip. She's my dog. If I go out of the room or out of the house without her, she won't move from where I've gone out until I come back. She just has to be near me.

Every morning and night when I go out to feed the animals she comes with me. I talk with her a lot. She's a real comfort and when we come in after going around the stock at night she'll come and sit on my knee. She almost purrs like a cat, she's so contented, apart from of course the occasional spat with Lottie.

I swear that if Peggy could talk she would probably tell me in words that she loves me. It isn't hard to work that out. I certainly love her and like I did with Pip I share all my thoughts with her.

Hold on though. On the other hand, it's maybe best she can't talk! Just kidding. She's my dog and I just love her to bits. Any dog owners reading this, you'll know exactly what I mean. They are just very special and are a part of you, aren't they?

Which brings me to Timmy!

He's a twat! A prize twat! This dog has been trouble from day one and he shows no sign of letting up. You might have guessed that I'm meaning that a little tongue-in-cheek, but what I'm telling you is no word of a lie. This dog really is T-R-O-U-B-L-E! You might well laugh, but he really is a little sod.

It all started with him in the womb!

Lottie is Timmy's mum from her third litter. She'd had three puppies from her first litter and one was so tiny when it was born, it was only the size of my thumb. We called him Tom Thumb and poor Tom had a right go at staying alive but just couldn't get there. He was trying his best to feed from Lottie but he was too small to even do that properly. Sadly, he was never going to make it and died at two weeks old, which was fourteen days longer than any of us had anticipated when we saw him that first time.

We weren't looking to be in the business of breeding dogs or becoming recognised Jack Russell breeders, but we sold the other two from Lottie's first litter to friends who still have them. They were both boys.

Lottie's second litter brought four puppies and we sold them to local friends and fellow farmers. We don't sell to anybody we are unsure about. I would be mortified to find that we had ever sold to someone who didn't look after our puppies. A local farmer James Edgar had one from us, Minnie, and I know she follows him wherever he goes and particularly enjoys James's favourite tipple, Guinness down at the Mended Drum in the village of Huby nearby.

We had thought of having one more litter off Lottie and maybe keeping a bitch off her, but life turned out a little different to that, thanks to Timmy. In fact life, you could say, has never been the same at Spring View Farm since this little pup arrived on the scene. Or to be more accurate, since he had chosen not to arrive. It had to have been him that was the cause of it, because Lottie was struggling.

She was having her litter and one pup had popped out no problem. It had arrived about 6 o'clock that Saturday night, but it got to 9 o'clock and nothing else had been born. We knew she was having four because we'd had her scanned. We rang our vets at Ripon as they have 24-hour service at Bishopton.

They told us that if she'd not had any more in

another hour to ring them again. Normally, going by the information available on the internet each puppy in a litter is born within 45 to 60 minutes after the previous one. If labour takes four hours between pups then you are advised to call your vet.

We had been three hours not four, so that extra hour made sense even though we were both starting to get really concerned. When it got to 11 o'clock and Lottie had still only had the one pup we rang again and they said to bring her in.

Of course, what you're thinking by then is that your travel time adds to the four hours that have already gone. Because of where we are the journey was going to take at best just over half an hour, but any traffic problems could easily take us to an additional hour. That would make it five hours since Lottie had the first pup. Poor thing – and we feared for the lives of the pups still inside her.

I'd like to say it was just Kate that was in a flap but we definitely both were. We set off from Thornton on the Hill just gone 11 o'clock and got to Ripon just before midnight.

Because this was in the midst of the first wave of Covid in the spring of 2020 we couldn't go into the practice. We just had to stay in the car park and had to hand over Lottie with the one pup she'd had a lot earlier that evening.

There was nothing we could do for her ourselves. If she was to need a caesarean she would have to stop overnight anyway. There was nothing we could do but come home and leave them to it and hope that Lottie and her three remaining pups, if they were still alive by then, would be okay.

It was a quiet car as we made our way back to Spring View Farm. You feel all kinds of emotion when something like this happens and mostly you feel in some way responsible. If we hadn't let her have a third litter this wouldn't have stood a chance of happening. But it had and suddenly you feel guilty.

It was a long couple of hours or so but the practice rang us a little later to say they had tried manual means to get the puppies out before conducting an emergency caesarean. The good news was that all four puppies were now out and mum and pups were all alive and well. Thank goodness for a 24-hour service!

And that meant Timmy was with us.

We didn't know it at the time, but he'd had his leg back in the puppy sac, not the way it should have been, and maybe that had something to do with Lottie not giving birth to him and the other two naturally.

Lottie had three boys and one girl from that litter and we had sold them all, but someone must have known about Timmy because they gave backword and so Timmy became dog number four of our troupe.

He is always riving about somewhere, he's always busy. He just never stops. He's always trying to dig something up in the garden or destroy a plant. He's industrious, I'll give him that, but mostly on destruction. He's the canine equivalent of a wrecking ball. He really is a terror, or probably even more accurately a terrorist! In fact, that's exactly what he is – a terrierist!

He is the first boy Jack Russell we have ever had as a pet and we haven't had him castrated and probably won't as we might end up using him as a dog for others' bitches. Just what his offspring will be like though, God only knows!

He's on a mission to kill himself, I know that much. It was Kate who noticed blue poo in the garden one day! Timmy had only eaten the rat bait! Oh my! That involved our first of two recent trips to the vet, but the second was far more serious.

It was late December, between Christmas and New Year. I came home from Green's at Thirsk and made myself a sandwich and a cuppa. Before I did that I'd fed the dogs.

I don't often go and sit down in the other room to have a bite and a brew and relax a little, but I was tired and had decided that before going out to feed the stock I'd have a bit of time to myself, watch a bit of telly.

I must have been in there about 20 minutes when I decided to go back into the kitchen and our main living area with the dining table and the sofas and armchairs beyond looking out into the garden. I don't know why I had gone back, maybe for a second brew or for a slice of cake.

Whatever the reason was soon became pretty academic.

On the floor next to the island unit and surface in our kitchen was an empty box where once there had been a Terry's Chocolate Orange.

It didn't dawn on me at first, the trouble that was to follow. I just thought that was strange, how had it got there? At this point it was no more than that, just a passing thought.

Then, a bit further along on the floor I saw the wrapping, the foil. A few bits here, bits over there, it was like a paper trail leading through from the island in the kitchen, past the dining area to the conservatory area and the sofas and armchairs.

And there, in the conservatory, was Timmy!

He's eating the very last segment of the chocolate orange! I was absolutely horrified! Beside myself with fear. Everybody who has a dog knows that chocolate and dogs don't go.

I quickly moved to try and grab the last segment from him, pretty futile really because he'd already eaten all the rest, but of course Timmy just devoured it even more quickly. I looked at this Jack Russell puppy and you should have seen his tummy. It was almost as though someone had put a football inside him.

That bloody chocolate orange had been on our island in the kitchen. It was out of reach. Or at least we thought it was meant to be. We had discovered Timmy could jump on to a dining room chair and from there he could get on to the dining room table to pick up scraps left from meals rather than waiting for them to drop below.

What we hadn't known was that he had found a bloody way of getting from the kitchen table to the island surface. He was obviously in training to be either our next Olympic triple jump or long jump medallist, the next Jonathan Edwards or Greg Rutherford. How he did it I don't suppose we will ever know but one thing was for sure: none of that mattered.

All that mattered was that our little lad, twat that he was, was in real danger.

I went into a wild panic because I knew this would kill him if I didn't act fast, and I might already have been too late.

Chocolate is poisonous to dogs because it contains a lethal chemical called theobromine that they are unable to metabolise. It can kill and there are equations of how many ounces of chocolate in relation to the dog's body weight that can be consumed whereby a dog may survive, but this little dog had stuffed himself with 157 grams! That's 5 and a half ounces! He was already way over any guideline that might have been regarded as offering hope.

It's amazing how clear everything becomes when you are definite about something and I knew that Timmy was going to die if I didn't do something straight away. But first I rang Kate.

'Get him to the bloody vet NOW!' were her words. Clear as crystal.

I rang the nearest vets I could think of, Bishopton again, but at Easingwold. Ten minutes away. I explained to the receptionist what had happened and that I needed

Timmy seeing urgently and why, but the receptionist said she was really sorry but there was no vet around. I can't remember whether it was something to do with Covid or some other issue. It was at Christmas after all, but the clock was ticking for Timmy. The receptionist suggested I go to Ripon, where Timmy had been born.

Time was not on my side. Ripon! It'll take me an hour! I think she got the desperation in my voice. It wasn't her fault though. She couldn't magic someone up who wasn't there. I rang Kate back. I told her we had a problem and to go and see Julian (Norton) who had started up a new veterinary centre not far from Green's at Thirsk where Kate was still working.

I set off towards Thirsk with Timmy but without any definite knowledge that Julian or any vet would be available. If there was nobody at least I was halfway to Ripon, but the only thing was I didn't know how long I'd got. I had no idea how soon Timmy might be affected.

I'm a mile away from home heading towards Thirsk when the lady at Bishopton Vets in Easingwold rings back. She tells me that she's got a veterinary nurse who can handle what needs to be done via a Zoom call with a vet at the other end. We will get Timmy sorted she says. Result! I say, brilliant! I'm on my way! And I turn the car around.

I'm a mile the other side of where we live when the phone goes again! It's Kate. She tells me it's all sorted. Julian's here. He'll do it. This is all very well – and I know Kate has been giving it her all and Julian has offered to do it, which is great, but Timmy's clock so far as I'm concerned is ticking. I tell Kate that I can't turn around again. I'm now only about seven minutes away from Easingwold.

Kate says that I can't do that, she's just told Julian I'm coming. I said I was sorry but I had to get Timmy to the nearest vet. The only thing on my mind was to get him to Easingwold, get Timmy out of the car and to the veterinary nurse.

Once again I handed over Timmy to Bishopton Vets, this time as a puppy rather than still in his sac ready to be born. If it had been pretty serious before he was born it was even more so now. I thought about never wanting to see a Terry's Chocolate Orange ever again. Once again I couldn't go into the veterinary practice, but this time I stayed, in the car park.

This bloody dog! But, you know, they all become part of you and Timmy was just that. He might be trouble, he might be a bit of a menace, he might make a mess of our plants, but he's our Timmy when all is said and done. And my God, does he have character in abundance.

Fifteen minutes later, out this little lad comes, tail wagging, strutting his stuff and acting as though nothing was ever wrong.

The nurse said she had got every segment out of him. I don't think it was because she knew how many segments are actually in a chocolate orange, more that she had located every single one. There are twenty by the way. I looked it up.

Every single segment was intact, none had dissolved. Timmy had just swallowed them down whole. The nurse had given him some kind of crystal to make Timmy vomit the segments and it had done the trick.

The nurse also gave me some charcoal liquid to give Timmy in his feeds over the next twelve hours in case there was anything left in his tummy that would cause some kind of reaction.

I thanked the nurse so much for what she had done – and took my twat of a dog home. I swear he was laughing at me as we made our way back to Spring View, but you know what, I couldn't have cared less. He might be trouble and he might be a bit of a twat, but Timmy was alive! Fantastic!

CHAPTER 5

TRACTORS

The Day I Lost My Ring

It was a very bright sunny day one crisp October morning. I'd been down to some land we rent about two miles away from Spring View at Newburgh Priory. The cattle were coming home, ready to be housed for the winter.

I was in my trusty tractor. It's a green Deutz Fahr tractor and I had a trailer on the back. I was picking up a ring feeder from the field. It's a heavy steel structure in the shape of a ring that you put hay and silage bales inside so that the cattle don't fight each other for it if it is just left loose in a field and it keeps it in one place. The animals put their heads through the gaps in between the metal structure to eat the hay.

If you're moving cattle out of the field there's no need for the ring feeder to be there, so that was my job on this sunny day. I felt great. Farmer Chris in his tractor, one of those lovely autumn days where everything seems right with the world.

Now the normal way to load a cattle ring feeder with a diameter of around 7 feet on to a trailer would be to unbolt the two sections that see it split into two easier halves. By doing it that way it makes it easier to load and also far safer.

My thought? You know what? I don't really need to take it apart. I've only a short distance to get back to the farm. I'll just take it in one go, just as one whole ring. I'll lift it into the trailer, go easy, it's a nice day, watch the world go by as I take it home. We live down very quiet country lanes. Nothing much comes traffic wise. It'll be okay.

Had I thought this through?

I lifted up the ring feeder with the loader on the front of my tractor and took the feeder to the trailer I'd left in the field. It didn't fit quite snugly. It was a bit too big, but it was a wonderful day, I was feeling good, nothing could possibly go wrong on a bright, sunny day like this.

My trailer has wooden sides. They would keep it reasonably stable. It was at an angle in the trailer, a bit skew-whiff, but if I drove carefully all would be well. I ran the tractor back around to the front of the trailer, hitched it on, and off we went.

I'm about half a mile away from the main road, which is nothing more than a country lane. All good. I'm taking it easy working my way from the field.

I've reached the end of the farm track and it's a left turn to go up the Coxwold to Oulston road. I pull out on to the country lane and start tootling up the road. It's all going well.

It's in a matter of a few seconds that I realise the road is on a gradient. Now the thing is you don't realise how much of a gradient it is until you are either running, as Chris Berry would say, or until you have added extra load to your normal travel with a tractor.

I'm aware of a slight change in my travel time, but I'm blissfully unaware of my impending state of mind, which is due to become all too clear very shortly.

I'm still tootling away thinking how the world is so wonderful, how joyous it is to be a farmer, when not one but two things change my day completely. First, the steering decides to go on my tractor. What?! Second, I change gear to gather speed to go up the hill on the basis I need to get up the hill and back to the farm before anything goes any further wrong.

But those two occurrences are nothing in comparison to what met my eyes as I turned around to look behind me!

I'd done so because in changing gear I had slightly jerked the tractor.

There, behind me, I saw my ring disappear. You couldn't make this up. It was real. The jerk of changing gear had dislodged the cattle feeding ring from its admittedly less than secure resting place in the trailer. As I had turned I had seen it falling off the back of the trailer that was still going uphill. The ring, now free from its temporary trailer residence, suddenly developed a life of its own.

It didn't just fall off and land flat on its base and lie there in the lane, oh no, it became a sodding wheel! Half a tonne's worth! And heading down the hill I'd just come up! I could feel my face go white as the horror of the situation took hold.

The beautiful village of Coxwold was a mile away, but at least this was a quiet country lane, nothing much comes down here or at least not too often. Hopefully it would stay that way.

Nope! As I'm looking over my shoulder, powerless to do anything that will stop this huge runaway steel ring, designed to withstand several half tonnes of nuzzling beasts, it suddenly gets ten times worse!

A white van appears!

Oh ... My ... God!

Nooooo!!! Surely this can't be happening? I can see the absolute horror on the poor man's face! The ring feeder is picking up a little pace as it rolls in his direction. I can literally feel my face going white with fear. What a stupid man I am. Why didn't I just unbolt the ring and put it safely on board the trailer in two pieces. Why, in God's name, did I not at least tie it down in some way?

Fortunately for me, and no doubt fearing any impact, the white van man had the presence of mind and a mean self-preservation instinct to put his van into reverse to avoid the ring smashing into him. If I hadn't been so traumatised watching the events unfold I would have seen the humour in it like some kind of comedy film scenario, but all I could see was my ring feeder rolling down the road and him there.

It wasn't over, because there was nowhere for white van man to pull off this little country lane and get out of the way. The ring feeder was still heading his way.

But there must be a God because for some reason, maybe a kink in the road, the ring veered off on to a grass verge and into a massive hedge just a few metres short of the van.

Thankfully the driver of the van, only a young lad of maybe 19, saw the funny side of what had happened and just pulled up alongside me making sure I was okay while laughing his head off. I can imagine him in the pub later that day telling his mates that they'd never believe what had happened!

After he'd gone I put my head in my hands. All I could think was how lucky I had been and that somebody must have been looking down on me. But I still had to get this ring feeder home and we still had well over a mile to go.

Hindsight is a wonderful thing. I should have unbolted it, put it on the trailer in two halves and then secured it in some way with either a big strap or roped it. I'd just banged it on the trailer, a ring that was too big and hadn't even tried to make it safe. I was only going two miles. The health and safety police would have had a field day with me!

Can you imagine if it hadn't been the white van with a young feller, but instead had been a little old lady or man in a saloon car who might not have reacted as quickly? This thing would have hit the vehicle, could have rolled right over it and who knows what would have happened to the driver or any passengers.

I would have been done for insecure loading and even manslaughter!

Imagine drawing a plan for any insurance claim. There's the tractor, trailer and the ring feeder all trundling along up this little hill. You then draw a little picture of the ring jumping off the trailer and travelling downhill to crush this Ford Fiesta or something like it. I'm not trivialising, I'm tormented by it! Imagine cyclists! They come around in big groups on these country lanes and regularly use this one.

'Farmer Chris wipes out old lady' or 'Local farmer slays 15 cyclists with runaway ring' would no doubt have seen an early end to my career as a farmer and these books would certainly have never seen the light of day.

Until I started this book I'd not even told Kate about this, in fact I still haven't! There was until now only me, Chris Berry and the van driver who knew this story! That's how terrified and embarrassed I was!

CHAPTER 6

TRACTORS

The Snow Plough

The weather plays such an important part in every decision a farmer makes every day of the year. Farmers have so many tasks that need undertaking and a lot is driven by what is falling down from the sky or which way the wind is blowing. I get why some farmers see a fantastic morning, all blue skies and sunshine, and don't do what they were going to.

Our first winter hadn't seen us suffer too much at the hands of the weather. It had been wet and windy, but not too bad. Our farm is situated 400 feet up and we face due south, which means the farm is susceptible to south-westerlies that can be very strong at times.

We'd had wet winters for the first few years and we'd had water stood in the fields for months. That's why pigs and cattle are generally brought in at winter. There is no sense in having livestock paddling around in the wet, it's poor husbandry. There is also little sense in it because you need that grass to be able to grow to feed the cattle and sheep when they graze in spring.

Our sheep stay out all year round because they graze on the higher ground.

We hadn't had any real snow until the winter of 2019–2020. Our country lane is fairly remote, a bit off-grid, and it doesn't take a lot to make it unpassable when snowdrifts load up the lane when they are blown in. It makes you realise how we can so easily get cut off. It's about quarter of a mile to another country lane at one end of the lane that passes our farm and a mile the other way. They're all single-track roads, but ours is the most remote.

That year we were snowed in for the first time. I loved the fact that we had enough of our own meat in the freezer and that I could get through the snow because I had a tractor! I could see other people having to walk down the lane and must admit I was chuffed that I could get out and go anywhere I wanted. It was a fantastic feeling.

When it had drifted even higher I decided it was time to make a snow plough! Well, I had to get to the pub somehow!

Get ready. You should know what's coming by now. Had I thought this through? I can guess your answer.

I had a loader on my tractor. It has two steel tines. Great big prongs to those that don't know. I had spare pallets that had been used for delivering animal feed and agricultural equipment from Green's. One of those would do the trick. I got hold of some plywood.

I made this snow plough. Hmm.

I only took it out once. That was enough. All that happened was that I just created the most humongous amount of snow in front of me. I actually made things worse! I obviously didn't have the technical know-how, but at least I had tried!

Instead, I satisfied myself being able to get down to the pub in my tractor while others could not. The only problem was when I got there it was closed!

CHAPTER 7

PIGS

Our First New-Born Pigs

I love pigs. I always have. Granddad had them, my dad had them, I'd had a go with them in my teens. I'd studied pigs at college, had worked on farms and had been a pig farm manager down south with my first wife and then up in East Yorkshire.

When we took on Spring View I just had to have some. I'd never thought about which specific breed I was going to have. All I knew was that I wanted coloured pigs rather than white and that was because they would be nicer to look at. It's quite important to me. I get real enjoyment from looking at my pigs. I don't mean to offend those who like white pigs but for me once you've seen one white pig they all look the same.

I wasn't looking to be a commercial breeder of any form of livestock. Our farm isn't big enough for that even now when we farm across 40 acres including land we now rent as well as own.

In the summer of 2015 we knew we were going to be taking on Spring View. Kate and I enjoy going to the Great Yorkshire Show at Harrogate. It is one of the biggest and best agricultural shows in the country, but I'm not one of those who likes to be there for the beer and I've never been great with big crowds.

Kate loves the Great Yorkshire Show and is much more of the party animal than I am. She used to love showing sheep at the show and is looking forward to doing it again soon, but she also loves the partying just as much, as she will tell you!

Since I've got older I've found this weird thing, that I don't really do crowds. It's different if I occasionally go to a concert. I can cope with that. The last time I went to something like that was to a Kylie Minogue concert!

I love Kylie and I took my friend's daughter to see her in Manchester. I've seen her three times, once in Leeds Arena and the other time in Paris with my second wife when we went on Eurostar.

But I've got worse with big crowds since the last time in Manchester.

It's nothing to do with the past few years and any fear of Covid, although I have been careful and we have been resolute at Green's, but it has turned out that the restrictions brought about through Covid have suited me as I haven't had to go out and mix with people as much in crowds.

I don't know whether it's a phobia or some kind of fear, I just don't like to be with tens of thousands of people.

I don't mind hundreds of course, manageable numbers if you ever come to visit my farm when I'm putting on an open day!

When it comes to going somewhere like the Great Yorkshire Show I want to be there at 7 o'clock that morning and on my way home by 2 in the afternoon. I want to be there, get at it, see what I want to see and getting home before all the madness starts. I'm like that in nearly anything I do. I'm very much a morning person.

I had gone to the Great Yorkshire Show this time because I was already thinking of buying some pigs for our new farm. I knew this was the place where I would be able to take a look at all the coloured pig breeds and that I would find some that would fit the bill.

I saw the Oxford Sandy & Blacks come out into the pig ring and both Kate and I fell in love with them. The plum pudding pigs as they are known, ginger and black.

We didn't buy any at that time as we were still considering what breed we might have, although we also fell in love with Whitebred Shorthorn cattle at that show and did something about that almost immediately.

Our first pigs at Spring View weren't Oxford Sandy & Blacks. They were 9 Berkshire crossbred weaners that I think I had found available on the website Preloved. They arrived 5 days after we took on the farm fully, in a blue horse trailer (that's Kate's memory for you, I have trouble remembering what I've gone into another room for, let alone remembering the colour of a horse box!). If you're keeping count that meant that now we had 50 ewes, a tup, 9 crossbred pigs and cattle numbers that you will find out in another of these tales.

On 14 November, just a week after the Berkshire crosses had come, our first Oxford Sandy & Black arrived, Elsie. We had bought her as a weaner from a farmer in the East Riding of Yorkshire. Elsie was to be the first step towards where we are today running a pedigree herd.

It was fantastic having pigs on the farm. I was in my element, back with where it had all started for me.

The Berkshire crosses were about 12 weeks old when they had arrived and we took them through to finishing, roughly another 12 weeks when we sold seven of them through Thirsk livestock market as prime pigs. We had decided to keep two of the girls (gilts) to breed from.

We had no breeding going on at this point. It was just a matter of having pigs, feeding them and managing them. Elsie was too young to breed from at that time, but we had visions of breeding in the near future.

It was the Great Yorkshire Show of 2016 that proved the real start of our work with the Oxford Sandy & Black breed. This time we did buy a pig at the show from a chap who had come up from Somerset to show his pigs. Somerset is a hotbed of Oxford Sandy & Black rearing.

When people go to the Great Yorkshire Show with their livestock they are there to show and hopefully do well, but they are also there to sell stock. And this was where we bought Gloria, who was ready to be served as Elsie now was.

Gloria was delivered to us by local livestock haulier specialists Bell's of Thirsk, after having been shown at Harrogate, and we were ready to roll!

I now had two young pedigree sows ready to be put to the boar, but we didn't start with an Oxford Sandy & Black boar. We bought a Pietrain boar from a farmer called Daniel Thackray from Blubberhouses. The Pietrain is a Belgian breed that is known for its production of lean meat and at the time we bought him the breed's reputation was on the up, which it still is today.

Our Pietrain boar served both Elsie and Gloria not long after we had bought Gloria that July and we were on our way. Funnily enough in those early years of being here I never once saw either a boar, bull or tup doing the deed and so my breeding programme was based more on hope than any guarantee of expectation, but I was soon able to see more sows were coming on nicely.

It was wonderful to be back working with breeding pigs. I thought back to certain times in the past when I'd worked for others on their pig farms in sometimes appalling conditions inside in stalls and on slats and was determined our pigs were going to be looked after better than anyone's.

I had my beautiful Oxford Sandy & Blacks outside, where the breed belongs as nature intended. It's where the pigs can display all of their characteristics, including rooting and just enjoying a happy life.

I loved it. The pigs were on lush green grass in the corner of a field, in my brand-new pig paddock with new fresh stakes, shiny new stock fencing and shiny new gates on the perimeter and pig arcs for shelter. Everything was lovely and rosy.

The green grass didn't last very long because pigs are the most destructive creatures that you can imagine and have this habit of rooting up anything and everything they possibly can and destroying the soil. Before long all this lovely grass had gone and they had turned it to mud.

I wasn't shocked. That's how pigs are when they are outside in their natural habitat. If a pig wants to root it roots. If it wants to eat worms it roots them out.

During the summer months when the sun rays are at their strongest, pigs can get sunburnt, which is why a wallow, a shallow water mud bath either made by the pigs' own rooting or manmade, is used by them forming a muddy form of sunscreen or just somewhere to cool off if the weather gets too warm. I made one for them.

But rain on an already rooted area, which is by now basically mud, does both the pigs and the land no real good. It can also make it very difficult to feed them, make sure they have water, clean bedding or even to move them and that's why I always bring them inside when the weather gets bad.

Our first sows were due to farrow, as any sows do when impregnated, in around 3 months, 3 weeks and 3 days, which would make them ready to farrow around mid-November and so I had brought them down into the livestock shed at the end of October when the clocks go back at the end of British Summer Time and the dark nights come. That's when I have them in loose housing and bedded on straw.

I hadn't wanted them farrowing up in the field and too far away from the farmhouse. I was thinking of Kate of course, as then it wouldn't be too far for her to walk with a torch in the middle of the night! She could always then come and get me if I was really needed, couldn't she? And you think I'm joking? I'll leave you to make your own mind up.

I had made an area within the shed and had brought one of the arcs from the field making an area where both the sows could farrow when their time came. They both farrowed within 3–4 weeks of each other.

Elsie was first to farrow in mid-November; Gloria farrowed in mid-December. Elsie had 6 piglets and Gloria had 8, which is alright but nothing like commercial units where sows generally farrow an average of around 12 pigs. This was both gilts' first time and they are rare breed, which means they have not been genetically modified to produce greater numbers regularly.

We now had even more stock, but more importantly to me there is nothing nicer or cuter that I have ever seen than a new-born Oxford Sandy & Black pig. They are just beautiful.

Piglets are the most amazing little creatures you can imagine. What many people don't realise is that the size difference between a new-born piglet and its mother is enormous. When they are born they are between 150-1 and 200-1 in size ratio to their mother. The sow often weighs something like 200 kilos, which is over 30 stone! The piglet weighs around 1.3 kilos.

They are often no bigger than my hand, but they are tough little things and within seconds of being born they are trying to get round to one of the sow's teats. It is amazing to watch the instinct of this tiny little thing that has just popped out, covered in birthing juices, and trying to suckle its mummy. It is one of the most wonderful, magical things I have ever seen and I am in awe every single time.

But we weren't quite there yet in having a new-born pedigree Oxford Sandy & Black because these had been sired by a Pietrain boar.

CHAPTER 8

PIGS

Lulu – The Clumsy Sow

Watching lots of piglets coming out of their mother and seeing them all suckling into the sow's teats is always one of those magical moments for me, but it is also the most dangerous of times for these little ones because of the difference in weight between piglet and sow, and the risk of the sow quite simply laying on them without realising.

Cindy, one of our current Oxford Sandy & Black gilts and homebred has recently produced the best litter we have ever had. She had 14 piglets. Sows generally have 14 evenly placed teats, but she has 16! I was there watching her have them at 2 o'clock in the morning and I said to Kate that her litter was never going to survive because they were all so tiny, but what a mother she is as all except one survived and did really well.

Cindy is lovely. I can go and talk to her, stroke her and she loves it.

Lulu, on the other hand, was a completely different matter. There was no question that she was productive. She produced the biggest litter we've had with 15 piglets, but that's where it ended. Just because a sow can produce a large litter doesn't mean it is going to stay that way.

Lulu was also the world's clumsiest sow. She squashed 7 of them to death. She was also a horrible old sow, not a nice pig at all. When they started growing she would even go and fight with them, knock them off their food. She was a real bully. She was greedy and very fat.

Within two or three days and with colostrum inside them it is surprising just how quickly they can move, but that was something the surviving eight of Lulu's litter probably learned quicker than most.

This was the second time Lulu had seen off about half of a litter and I decided that although there was no doubt she was a prolific birthing sow there was very little benefit in it if she was going to crush half of them to death.

Lulu wasn't just clumsy but nasty. It was time for her to go.

CHAPTER 9

COWS

Our First Whitebred Shorthorns

All I knew for absolute definite when we were getting our little corner of heaven here at Spring View Farm was that I wanted cows.

I couldn't wait to have cattle and both Kate and I had made the decision that whatever it was we were going to have on the farm needed to be that little bit special, something different, something really pleasing on the eye, something that was a friendly, easy-to-handle breed.

I wanted to do something with a rare breed, something that we could be proud of in doing our bit to help maintain and expand the numbers of whatever breed we chose.

Our decision was made far easier by going to the Great Yorkshire Show in July 2015.

When Kate and I go to the showground in Harrogate where this fantastic show is held we always enjoy going on the Rare Breeds Survival Trust stand. You can see rare breeds being shown in the cattle rings, but there is always so much more information you can get from farmers of rare breeds and many of them go on to the stand to be available to talk to others or encourage new rare breed farmers.

At the 2015 Great Yorkshire Show we saw what will always remain as a radiant picture in my head. It was this beautiful scene of a white cow and her calf. I didn't know what the breed was at the time, but Kate knew instantly. Her dad had a Whitebred cow as their house cow, that she had milked.

This cow and its calf were simply stunning and we introduced ourselves to their owner, breeder Helen Chard from near Burnley.

While we were fairly well smitten by Helen's cow and calf, we didn't make a decision there and then, at Harrogate, over going into the breed. We did a little bit of research first into others. We wanted to be certain that Whitebred Shorthorns were for us.

We looked into other white breeds. Funny that. I didn't want a white pig because I'd felt once you'd seen one, you'd seen them all, but when it came to cattle that's exactly what I felt happiest with. But pure white or close to pure white breeds of cattle are certainly not what you tend to see every day.

Our shortlisted breeds that we then looked into a little further were the British White and White Park, both excellent breeds, but there was something about the Whitebred Shorthorn breed that had already struck a chord in our hearts, and it was rarer than the others.

Kate puts it slightly differently, and probably more accurately:

"The Whitebred Shorthorn has a better shape. It is a dual-purpose animal and although we don't milk our cows, even though you can because they are very milky, they are more commonly used as a beef animal and a Whitebred Shorthorn bull is known for being perfect for crossing with many breeds.

"It is often referred to as a simply a White Shorthorn and became best known for crossing with the Galloway to produce the well-respected Bluegrey crossbred. Many years ago it was also known as the Cumberland White.

"For me, that bit more shape to the cows than the British White or the White Park is what makes the difference, and most importantly they were in our price range. If we had gone into other Shorthorns like the Beef Shorthorn or Dairy Shorthorn we would have had to pay a lot more money for our stock – and they are not rare breeds."

Kate's right. On both counts. The Whitebred Shorthorn certainly has a lovely shape – and as we'd sunk everything into buying this place we had to be careful with money.

It had been a massive achievement to buy this little farm, and whilst we are on that tack I have to mention Sue Huffington of HSBC.

Sue was our bank manager at the time and has been a marvellous supporter of us as a couple through our business life. Sue could see just how much getting this place meant to us and without her we might not be where we are today.

Sue gave us fantastic advice over how to achieve what we were looking to do, and we couldn't just buy anything, even though it looked as though that's exactly what I was doing.

We made up our mind. It didn't take us long and I think that really, we knew as soon as we'd seen them, we were going with the Whitebreds.

The Rare Breeds Survival Trust has the Whitebred Shorthorn on its watchlist with only around 150 registered pedigree breeding cows, and so far as I was concerned that meant we would be getting into a breed where we could do some good, help it prosper or at very least not see it slide away.

With rare breeds it is vital to keep the long-standing bloodlines going and that's why it is important to get to know the other breeders and what they have.

In any breed of any species of animal you need good sire lines and good dam lines but if you haven't much to play with in the first place you have to make sure that what still exists is carried on.

Having had that initial contact with Helen at Harrogate we went over to see her Haylot herd in Lancashire within a couple of days of the show and bought two cows Lochdochart Snowfall 19 and Berscar Snowfall that were soon to become known to us simply as Lochie and Bertha. And they were both in-calf.

As we were four months away from moving into Spring View we hadn't anywhere for them and so Helen looked after them for us until we were ready.

They arrived on the farm on November 15, 2015, within a fortnight of us coming here and I could not have been more pleased. This was the moment I had been waiting for. My own cows, my own cattle, the start of my own herd. I was starting to feel like a real farmer.

Bertha and Lochie were to have great stories with us and were to mean so much to me and to Kate, but they took time to settle. They were clearly on edge for the first month or two. They were obviously used to being with Helen and she had wintered them outside.

We didn't have the land to be able to offer them that opportunity here. So, they had suddenly been transported from Lancashire to Yorkshire and had been put inside a building rather than being out on grass. Quite a change from what they had been used to, and a new person looking after them.

When I went in to see them I could see in their eyes they were saying, 'What are we doing here?' and 'Who are you?'

But one of the great things about a farmer and his animals is that relationship you develop. Once they get to know you, having built up their trust, they are completely different and that's how it was with our girls. I would go in and talk with them and stroke them.

These beautiful white cows became our friends – and helped us build our herd.

CHAPTER 10

CALVES

The Calves That Wouldn't Get Up

Lochie and Bertha were my pride and joy. They weren't quite our first official pedigree animals on the farm as Elsie, our Oxford Sandy & Black pig had arrived just two day earlier, but they were different, far different, big beautiful cows that looked terrific.

We weren't sure when they were going to calve and here's another thing that suddenly came to mind. I'd farrowed a pig, I'd lambed a ewe, but I'd never calved a cow in my life! Guess what? You're right, I was starting to think this through!

I'd never thought about this until it dawned on me as calving was approaching, although Kate said she probably had on her dad's farm when she was younger. I'd worked on a dairy farm where calves were born but not actually been there if I'd been needed.

Since our first calvings in 2016 we've had many a day or night when we've had to calve on our own and I'm telling you there have been some hairy moments.

Keeping cows is not for the fainthearted. They are big animals that can weigh up to around 1000 kilos and when they are pregnant, about to have a calf, their baby, you've got to be there on hand, sometimes to help them.

Did we have any handling system for them? I think you know the answer.

Kate will now tell you what happened that first time

when Bertha was first to calve. Our first calf to be born at Spring View. Quite a momentous event, but at the wrong time of day. I'm a morning person, but this was just out of kilter slightly.

"Our bedroom is at the front of the house and it has windows at three sides, one of which looks down on the shed where the cows were, only 30 yards away. You could see into the shed from our window.

"I woke up at 4 o'clock one morning and said to Chris, 'Your cow's calving, you'd better get up.' I knew he could hear me and was probably hoping I would go first and then come back and tell him if he was really needed. I know what he's like."

Yes, I had heard Kate, and yes, I was probably still in dreamland, probably dreaming about having a herd of 100 cows, a flock of 500 sheep and 50 breeding sows. Believe me that would be more of a nightmare than a dream for me today, as I now know my limitations and am totally happy with the stock we have.

But I did get up and I did get down there with Kate. We were both really excited about our first calves. I'd had hopes that we would maybe get two heifer calves, or maybe a heifer calf and bull calf.

The really great news was that our two old girls, Lochie and Bertha, knew what they were doing. They had both been around the block a bit and they both just popped out their calves.

Bertha gave birth to a bull calf and a few days later Lochie also gave birth to a bull calf.

But on that first day of calving when Bertha calved our world suddenly began turning upside down when the calf wouldn't get up!

One of the brightest things you want to see when a foal is born or a calf is born is the foal or calf fairly swiftly getting up on its feet. We had the same problem with

Lochie's calf too.

I'm thinking, this isn't right. These calves should be up and sucking and they're not. They were just lying there, both of them.

They eventually got up after about two hours, but it was very worrying. You see, that's what young stock does to you. It's like worrying about your babies when they are born. Anything that isn't right or doesn't go right you worry about.

We spoke with Helen and she said the calves in her herd had always laid flat for the first couple of hours.

We weren't going to let that kind of worry happen again though, and now we give a bolus and the calves are now much wicker, a lot sharper when born and get their heads up straight away and on to their feet in about half an hour.

It's funny but we had been selling boluses to farmers through Green's for so many years, but now we were able to tell customers that we had first-hand experience of how they worked for us. We're now much more knowledgeable about our products now that we have stock of our own.

Two bloody bull calves!

That wasn't going to get my herd going, was it? I had really wanted at least one heifer calf so that she could join the cows in the herd, but it wasn't to be and you have to be grateful for what you're given. We'd had two successful calvings, a little bit of stress along the way, but all was well.

We registered our herd prefix as Springview with the Whitebred Shorthorn Society and called one Springview Roxburgh and the other Springview Alexander.

Alexander is my youngest son's middle name and I did start by saying that Roxburgh had something to do with someone or other when Kate said this ... I'll let her tell you the way she told me. I think you'll like it, I certainly did.

"You're absolutely talking out of your bottom. When we went to Jamaica and you cut your foot the lady that helped you was called Roxy, so you said that when our cows calve I'm going to call a calf after you. As we were hoping it would be a girl we were going to call it Roxy, but it was a boy so we called it Roxburgh."

Ahem. Once again I bow down to my wife's better recall of events, but wait a second because how I cut my foot is another story.

What happened you couldn't make up. We were on holiday in Jamaica before we got the farm, something we can't do any more because we are here permanently now.

We were lying on sunbeds. It's 30 degrees, the most beautiful day. We'd been for a swim and were both relaxing. Kate was reading a book.

All of a sudden I could see things being blown off the beach. It was a whirlwind coming towards us.

It hit us! The sunbed went up into the air with me on it and I fell down. People all around were getting rocketed into the sky. It was the most incredible thing and only lasted what must have been seconds but in the time that it did it had been devastating..

I landed on something, or Kate reckons something, like a plastic chair had come down on me and I thought, 'My God, my foot is killing me.' I looked down and there was blood pouring from it. Kate said I was close to passing out.

This lovely American lady called Roxy came over and was my First Aider, then a guy arrived with a wheelchair from the hotel that had its own private surgery. Maybe these kind of events weren't unusual for it to have one!

I was cut on the right side of my right foot and I ended up having stitches in it.

That's how Springview Roxburgh came to be named, after the lady who looked after me.

And would you believe it, Springview Roxburgh went on to be a three-time champion at Cleveland County Show at Stewart Park in Middlesbrough; at Ryedale Show and at the Whitebred Shorthorn Breed Society Show and sale at Borderway Mart in Carlisle where we sold him for an amazing 2400 guineas to a farmer from Wales who used him on his Highland herd.

Not bad at all for a calf that wouldn't get up when he was born – and a lesson to me that bull calves can pay their way!

CHAPTER 11

SHEEP

Doris – The Kerry Hill

For Kate's 60th I bought her six Kerry Hill ewes, one for every decade of her life. I'm thoughtful that way. It wasn't long before we'd bought another six.

Kate had always wanted to have them. They are the most strikingly beautiful sheep with such clearly distinct black and white markings on their faces and legs. They began from a little town called Kerry on the English/Welsh border.

But we found out they were quite difficult to deal with and really quite wild. Although they weren't very easy to catch or handle, they did however produce some amazing lambs.

We put the success of our lambs down to having acquired a fabulous, top Kerry Hill tup from breed society chairman Linda Barnard.

This had been our second year of lambing since coming to the farm and I helped Kate when she had a big strong ewe to contend with. That's the time when you invariably need two people.

I would hold the ewe, keeping it steady, while Kate would help the ewe if it needed assistance. And just the same as when women have babies, cattle have calves, pigs have piglets, ewes have no idea what time of day their lambs are going to be born.

If you ever hear of a sheep farmer putting people off coming to the farm for meetings or nearly any form of social activity it is nearly always because of lambing having gone through the night and into the next day for a month or in some cases many months.

While we only had those twelve ewes to lamb, you still didn't know when and so any other life you may have was generally put on hold during this time. Not so with us! One of us, at least, had to be over at Green's every day too, but like I said we only had a small number to lamb.

I recall that second year of lambing was a little bit easier if only because we had less ewes to lamb, plus we lambed a little later too.

One of the greatest pleasures that livestock men and women have is that time when there is new life on the farm whether lambs, calves or piglets and these sheep looked quite a special sight, especially when they got out of the buildings and into the fields.

The Kerrys lambed very well at a lambing percentage of 175 per cent, which meant that across the small flock of 12 ewes they had averaged one and three-quarter lambs giving us 21 lambs in total. Suddenly we were back with over 30 sheep on the farm.

Our original plan in having the Kerrys was that this might be the breed for us. We'd had Mules the first year's lambing and had then specifically chosen the Kerrys because Kate liked them. We'd thought that we could build up the flock from our good starting base by keeping some females back, but they were proving a little too lively, too hot to handle for us and we made the decision that we would go out of them and into another breed.

All of the fields had been properly fenced or refenced and so it wasn't a case of them getting away. It was just that they were not easy to gather up, difficult to deal with and to put it plainly they were a pain to handle and organise.

We had the male lambs castrated and their lamb went either through our new farm shop at Green's called Mrs Pumphrey's or we sold them privately. The ewe lambs we sold, along with the ewes to other Kerry Hill breeders.

There is definitely a healthy demand for the breed, it's just that they didn't suit us.

Well, one did!

When we bought the second six from a farmer it had meant to be five, but the farmer said he would throw in this old Kerry Hill ewe for thirty quid. That was the price he said he would get for her if she was culled. She was an old thing, bless her, and skinny but we bought her all the same.

We named her Doris.

Doris must have known we needed help because she became our sheepdog, because she followed the bucket and all of the other sheep followed her. She was around as our sheep journey continued, which saw us with Hebrideans and Shetlands before arriving, as we have now at the Border Leicesters.

Doris was with us for three years and both Kate and I loved having her around. We knew she was getting on a bit when we'd taken her on, but she had continued to produce lambs and we couldn't decide whether or not to put her into lamb in 2020.

It got to spring of last year, 2021, and she was in-lamb, but sadly she didn't make it. One day she just collapsed and that was it, she'd had enough. It was a sad day and we had to call our neighbour and also licensed slaughterman Cooper to come and put her to sleep. It was sad because she had been our pet sheep but at the end of the day where you have livestock you are also going to have deadstock.

But Doris lives on here at Spring View!

The previous year to her going Doris had had a ewe lamb – Baby Doris! She's a pure Kerry and she has just had her first lamb having been crossed with a Border Leicester. You see, there's always another life to come to a farm – but that takes nothing away from our love of our original sheepdog sheep Doris.

CHAPTER 12

COWS

Keep Away from the Mad Cow!

Exhibiting your animals at local agricultural shows during the summer is a very good thing to do. The public from all walks of life who come to an agricultural show love seeing the cows, bulls, calves, ewes, rams, lambs and pigs.

When you're showing your stock it involves a great deal of preparation beforehand, getting for instance the beast to walk slowly around a parade ring. If you've done your job properly beforehand and you have someone as adept at prepping your beast before going into the ring then you are likely to stand a better chance.

We attended Ryedale Show in 2016 with Bertha, but we didn't enter any classes.

We weren't where all of the livestock action was taking place. I'd decided it would be a good idea to take Bertha and her three-month-old bull calf Springview Roxburgh to the show, but that they would be on our Green's trade stand.

What a lovely idea! Our own cattle at the show. I was so proud and was looking forward to a gorgeous day showing off my cattle and talking with everyone about them, these beautiful Whitebred Shorthorns we now had.

Had I thought this through? Clearly not.

I'd done everything I could and thought that was right. Getting ready for a show of any kind takes an awful lot of preparation involving time and hard work. If you've a trade stand as we had, you've to get there early, usually at least the day prior to the show, cut the grass, make sure your marquee is set up properly and laid out the way you want it with appropriate refreshments for visiting customers.

We used to sell livestock handling equipment at Green's, so I'd taken these big cattle hurdles to the showground to make a temporary pen for Bertha and Roxy.

I'd had this romantic vision of taking my beautiful cattle and people just loving seeing them. They'd been washed and brushed and looked absolutely stunning. We made a lovely pen, bedded it with straw, put water in and we were ready.

This was going to be a great day! The weather was superb. A lovely sunny day. I'd made sure that they had some shelter from the sun by using the canopy of the marquee to provide cover.

We brought my favourite cow ever and her young bull calf on to the showground and into the makeshift pen early before the public arrived to make sure we could get on to the stand and unload them. They were settled in and absolutely fine.

I was now looking forward to my greatest day yet as a farmer and now pedigree cattle breeder. It all felt wonderful. I was happy with our preparation and I was delighted to be there. All I needed after all this work was to enjoy talking about my cattle, explaining about the breed and accepting compliments on our fabulous animals. A fantastic, stress-free day.

Unfortunately, nobody had explained this to Bertha!
She was an utter sod!

You know something? You never stop learning in life. And you never stop learning about animals and what you should or shouldn't do.

The thing is that when we bought our two cows our vision had been of the cow we had seen at the Great Yorkshire

Show, called Elizabeth, and her calf, standing serenely in the Rare Breeds Survival Trust marquee. My expectation, based upon that, had been that others would now have a similar experience to mine, that they would take one look at these beautiful cattle and fall in love with them.

But oh no! That's not the way it turned out at all. Whatever I may have thought or anticipated turned out to have been through rose-tinted spectacles of my Great Yorkshire Show experience.

From 9am that morning the show was busy everywhere. The crowds flooded in. Some talked of it perhaps even being the best-attended show ever. And it was a scorcher!

I hadn't reckoned on Bertha at all! She was very protective of her calves and she did not at all like the attention that was coming hers and Roxy's way. Remember Roxy was still only three months old and to be fair to Bertha she was only doing what she thought was right and looking after the best interests of her calf.

She began trying to attack anyone who came near! All this bloody cow wanted to do was kill anybody in sight and it was the children that seemed to anger and upset her most! Mercy me!

I was suddenly petrified that she was going to get out, get free of this spartan pen I had spent hours getting together, and go wild, running amok all around the showground. You do hear of this kind of thing happening from time to time at shows, but when it is your own beast it is a very different experience and you feel as though it is totally your responsibility to ensure it doesn't.

My day was officially in tatters! Stress-free day? No chance! Over my life there have been times when I have not coped well with stress and here I now was stressed beyond compare.

Rather than having taken a docile, placid, calm-natured Whitebred Shorthorn cow, it turned out I had turned up with something that resembled more of a raging bull!

I never moved from alongside her all day as I was that scared of what might happen and Bertha showed no real sign of cooling off. Maybe the heat didn't help either. She really did turn her hog out!

I had a massive job restraining her because of how unhappy she had become, not at all the placid, good-natured cow, if a bit of a monkey sometimes at home.

I just knew I had a duty to ensure I was there throughout as I was totally responsible for this animal being on the showground.

Obviously, the last thing I wanted was anyone to be injured, or worse. In the end I had to shield her off from general view and only give people a sneaky look at her and Roxy rather than have anyone approach her. It was just too dangerous.

I had to get a load of big banners and tie them all the way around her pen and even put up a sign saying KEEP AWAY FROM THE MAD COW!

The welfare of your animal should always be your top priority and I knew I had to get her off the showground as soon as I could, but with the show in full swing and something like 15,000 people, there was just no way and it was down to me to manage my situation.

This had been my first time ever taking an animal to any show. I'd thought how wonderful it would be. She would just stay there all day, munching hay, her calf would suckle on her udder and all would be hunky-dory.

By a short time into the show I was thinking very differently!

I thought if this is how it is going to be when showing an animal then we won't be doing it again, but as it turned out we did the very next year when Roxy became our first winner!

CHAPTER 13

IDIOT

The Gambler

The one thing that brought about our little farm is Green's, the country store that we have run at Thirsk livestock market since 2004. It has been the vital cog in our wheel and was the only reason we were able to move here, to build the great life we lead today.

And we were in danger of losing everything – Green's and Spring View Farm – when I not only took my eye off the ball but also began doing something that I am totally embarrassed about now.

It had been great fun buying animals and putting them on the farm. I was like a kid left to run free in a sweet shop. I was buying up anything I wanted, bringing it here and being the farmer I'd always wanted to be, but looking back I was also a bit of an idiot.

Kate was happy for me about being what I'd always wanted to be albeit in a small way and we were both really pleased with ourselves because of what we had done with the farmhouse, our new home. We had worked hard in transforming it from something that needed a lot doing to it, something that had been quite dilapidated

Kate was also happy because she was now able to have her own horse on her own farm, whereas before she had had to keep it in livery.

I had been taking down buildings on the farm, putting up new ones, putting up fences, renewing old fences, all things that needed to be done and it was taking over my time.

At the same time we were expanding or had expanded our business and had outlets at Northallerton and at Ruswarp Mart near Whitby, as well as having extended our premises at Thirsk.

Our overheads were on a massive increase. Staff numbers were on the up, we had more vehicles, we were taking on more stock.

What ended up happening was that everything that I had always controlled alongside Kate was getting out of control, but I had my farm. I was happy there. I was going into Green's at 7 in the morning to open up, check that everyone was there, doing their jobs and then it was Bye! I was on my way back to the farm by 9.30am.

All I had in mind was that I had all these jobs that I wanted to do on the farm, something that wasn't making us any income, and I had totally divorced myself from the day-to-day task of running Green's. I was absolutely passionate about being at Spring View Farm and making this into what I wanted it to be. My vision.

Looking back now it was like I'd left it all to Kate and the others we had employed to handle everything, that I'd basically said F***, I'm off to play farmers! It was my fault, I hold up my hands entirely.

We were basically paying some of our people to do the jobs that I had always done and should have been doing. We were paying out tens of thousands of pounds to people who were very good, but I should have been there. We had a really very good young man, very capable and at the top of his game, but it should have been me. We were paying people to move stock around the warehouse which I had always done before and I do again now.

Everything was bringing more pressure on the business and I wasn't helping. I'd abdicated responsibility. I turned a blind eye to it all. I just wanted to buy a tractor, so I bought a tractor. I wanted to buy some cows, so I bought some cows.

And where was the money coming from for all of this? Yep, Green's!

Before I tell what happened that left me ashamed, let me explain something. And this is by no means justifying what I did.

I've never been one to think about suffering from depression the way you hear it affects some people, but I have had mental health issues in the past, notably, if you read my first book, the time when I was going through hell and stood on the main York to Edinburgh railway line years earlier.

I got into gambling.

It was all within the first year and a half or so of being here. Everything was done on my iPhone and credit cards. And this was quite a serious habit. Kate knew nothing about it, so far as I knew.

I can't put my finger on why it happened but it may have been something I started when I had an operation on my big toe, which had left me laid up. I've had several operations on it since, but at that time it meant I was unable to do what I desperately wanted to do on the farm. I couldn't walk for a few weeks and was struggling.

I have a friend who gets tips on horses to bet on each day and at first I did really well. It was unbelievable. I was up by £10,000 at one time and I just thought this is great. This is going to help the farm. I can buy another cow. I'm a professional gambler. This is easy.

I had accounts with all of the major betting companies – Bet365, Paddy Power, Ladbrokes, Coral, about 10 apps in all. It's so easy to press buttons on your phone. A horse wins. You've won. In the top right of your screen you see all this money.

Welcome to my farm!

Welcome from both of us ...
on the farm

... and in our garden

I love pigs, me!

Kate loves horses. Here she is with Lorna

... and here's Kate riding out with Lorna

My first ever tractor. It's back in full working order at last!

My Whitebred Shorthorns – so proud!

Here's looking at you!

Now let me tell you about this year's calves!

One of the real joys of my life – new life on the farm

Young Bertha born 2022

How can
you not like
these?

Kate and me with our new sheep breed – the Border Leicesters

Look at this cracking ewe and lamb!

Kate's great with the Border Leicesters, born 2022

Feeding time, Kate-
style! Look at the mum
looking over!

Where's Julian so that we can try this again?

Oxford Sandy & Blacks born 2022

How can you not like these too?

Getting those jobs done!

Me and Timmy.
Got to love that dog

Kate and me with Peggy
and Poppy

Up our hill, looking for those bloody sheep!

All my ewes found! Happy Farmer Chris! See you soon!

I love flat racing. Kate and I used to own a racehorse but funnily enough I never gambled when we had him. He won too. When the flat racing season stopped I went on to jump racing. It got to the stage that at 10 o'clock at night in the wintertime and when Kate had gone to bed I needed something else to gamble on.

There might have been some South American football going on. I'd bung 50 quid on some correct scoreline. I'd get up the following morning and find I'd won. Brilliant. I began gambling on everything from darts to tennis.

I'd been up by big money, but now I was down by just as much and as it ended up before something was done, a great deal more. I maxed out all my credit cards.

I was hiding the credit card statements every time they came through the post. I had now got myself into a terrible state mentally.

It was Kate who found out. I'd better let her explain from here.

"I was struggling trying to hold everything together at Green's. We'd moved into this bigger place, the rent was enormous and there really was no money.

"I was juggling. I would pay one person but couldn't pay someone else. Then you can't get new stock because they won't let you have it as you haven't paid for the previous stock.

"Every Monday morning I just did not want to go in to work because I thought I was going to have to juggle more money. I had people on my back all the time. I just got on with it but it was horrendous.

"When I found out about Chris's gambling thing I just thought bloody hell! Chris didn't tell me. I found out. I went to him because he had left a bank statement on the worktop unopened and I thought, What's this?

"I opened it and when I saw all these payments to gambling companies I just thought, Oh my God!

"I thought, What do I do? I went to Chris and said, 'What's all this about?' And he said he needed me to sort it out. So I did. I sorted it. I'm a money juggler, after all."

Kate handled it all. I was down about £15,000 on my credit cards, having been up £20,000 at one time. I had lost £35,000 in the space of six months!

She was understandably absolutely horrified and obviously very upset. After all it had taken to get here. The hard work, blood, sweat and tears at Green's to get this beautiful place I'd wanted all my life I was tossing it all away for both of us.

Kate really wasn't that hard on me. She never is. She is such a lovely person. She helped me.

I hadn't stopped gambling when the cards were maxed out. I'd started taking cash out of the company too! I might not have been able to use the apps on my phone any longer but I owned the company where cash was still available to me and that became my new source.

I was going into Green's and then straight down to the bookies in Easingwold, but now lesser amounts of 50 quid here, 50 quid there. However, once Kate knew what I had been up to and my shame was out in the open everything stopped.

Kate took away all my credit cards and paid them off and from that moment on I have no longer had access to credit cards or our bank account. I've not gambled since.

I am lucky that I have a supportive wife and these days I can watch horse racing on television and enjoy it the way we did when we owned our racehorse. Strangely enough, I wasn't enjoying the racing when I was gambling.

I still feel terribly sorry for what I did and how irresponsible I was to leave Kate to do what she had to do at work while I gambled away our future. I was bleeding our business dry and at the same time heaping more and more stress on the one person who ended up getting me back right.

Whatever we have achieved since and whatever we achieve in the future is all down to what Kate did at that moment. Something had to give. Our marriage could have broken up, but it didn't and I will forever be grateful.

CHAPTER 14

GREEN'S

How We Saved the Farm

When we bought Spring View Farm and I was the farmer I'd always wanted to become it was as though I didn't really care about the business that had got us there, at least for a year or nearly two. My heart was in the farm, but my business head that I'd felt had served me well for many years was somewhere in the clouds.

Kate says: "All Chris ever wanted to do was get more and more business and get bigger and bigger." And Kate was right. But as anyone will tell you in business you can get bigger and bigger for a while using your same resources, which means you are not increasing your overheads because you can cope with it yourself or with the people that were involved when you had less business, but there comes a point when you have to expand in the property you are utilising and take on more people.

Unless you are clever enough to get that equation right you can find yourself going backwards.

There is a very old and very true saying in business that turnover is vanity and profit is sanity. And I hadn't been giving any thought to the profit. Turnover was going up and I just thought that meant we had to be making more money. I can tell you here and now that increasing your turnover does not work unless you are able to make the right margin and control your cashflow with enough coming in to keep everybody happy.

We weren't.

I had totally taken my hand off the tiller. What was even worse was that I had done it at a time when we had taken on more people than we'd ever had before. It might not seem a lot, but we had gone up to fifteen staff, which was a massive increase for us. We had three vans out on the road for deliveries. And I was at home on my farm!

I'd left Kate to run Green's. She was absolutely on her own in there after I had opened up and made sure everyone was in and then buggered off to the farm. It was like we were leading two separate lives. Kate would come in after me in a morning. I used to wait until she'd arrived, then I'd beat a hasty retreat.

I was spending way too much time here on the farm, which quite frankly wasn't creating any money whatsoever. All it was doing was spending money that we didn't actually have because I was taking money out of Green's and saying, F*** it, I want it, I'm going to have it. Everything will come right. How bloody naïve.

It was one of the most selfish things I've ever done. I was oblivious to the fact that my wife was going through hell, that she was as she says juggling money and that she was suffering. I was bleeding the business dry but even more importantly I was putting enormous pressure on Kate.

It was getting to Kate, as it would to anyone. She couldn't sleep. She was thinking about how she could pay one of our suppliers £20,000 for their milk powder one second and then how she was going to be able to pay £15,000 to another for animal feed blocks the next day.

Kate was understandably worried about everything, because it was all going tits up – and I didn't seem to care! I was the farmer now. I'll let Kate tell you what she thought now:

"Everyone needed paying and we didn't have the

money. I just thought, How am I going to pay all the wages at the end of each month? I can't pay! I haven't any money!

"I hated it. Chris has dragged me along behind him sometimes very reluctantly and on a very long string, but this was just too much."

I don't know how she did it or how she managed but Kate is resilient and she just gets on and finds a way no matter what it takes. So, if you come along to the farm having read this, be in no doubt about my wife. She is strong and tough and is the reason we are still here and farming.

Kate and I now work more closely than ever together, we live together and we farm together. That's not easy sometimes for a married couple to do, but I wouldn't have it any other way. We literally now do everything together.

But that's not all, by a long way.

In the early part of 2018 we were approached by a farm supply business called BATA who offered to buy Green's. It had come about through an agent who deals in buying and selling of companies. He'd mentioned previously that he'd had a company interested in buying us but it came to nothing. This time he said he had a company – BATA – who were really serious.

My instant reaction, given the state we were in at this stage, was, 'Thank God for that!'

I thought that this was it! We could sell the business, have loads of money in the bank, be able to pay off all the debt, retire and then just doodle about a bit at home on the farm while Kate could ride her horse as much as she wanted. Brilliant!

We had an initial meeting with our accountants and it all looked very straightforward. Our accountant Phil said something along the lines of: "I can't believe it. You two are the luckiest people in the world that this company is offering to buy your business."

I just saw an escape route from where we had come to, and I was on my way down that tunnel!

They were going to pay us this sum of money and we would be able to go off into the sunset, but as you might have guessed it didn't work out that way at all.

Our talks with our accountants and solicitors, with BATA and with their accountants and solicitors went on and on until May 2018. Due Diligence is the term that is well used in these matters and I had no idea what a huge undertaking it is. It's basically like stripping yourself off completely and letting them look at every part of you and scrutinise everything! Kate and I didn't get undressed by the way!

Every scrap of paper relating to anything, whether people, customers, suppliers, staff, stock, buildings, warehouses, offices, cabins, vans, cars, contracts, insurances, MOTs is looked over, pawed over, analysed. Every transaction, every document, every letter, text, email you have ever sent or received.

I'd thought at the outset this was going to be the answer to all of the problems we had been facing, but no. Instead, all we were racking up were even greater costs! It had got to around £12,000 in accountants and solicitors' fees by October 2018 and still there had been no deal done.

Kate hadn't been keen anyway when she heard what they were offering initially. She'd said it wasn't enough to give us the life we wanted. We had a mortgage here at the farm, which would still need paying, and we had loans within the business that related to the farm that would all have to be cleared as part of the deal that was being offered.

The figures they were talking about wouldn't have given us enough money. We might have just about managed to come away from the business with no debt but that would have been it.

I'd hoped that the due diligence and all of the time we had undertaken might have brought about an increased offer. After all, they had approached us in the first place. Surely they wanted Green's?

That summer I'd been convincing myself that everything was going to turn out alright, that BATA were going to buy us. We'd have money in our bank. We might have had to work for them for a while as a handover but we could cope with that. What a nice world I thought we lived in.

After nearly ten months since their initial approach we were asked to go to a meeting with BATA's accountants in Leeds. It was now October 2018. We duly went along with our accountants to conduct what we had hoped would be the final deal with hopefully an improved offer. We thought there might be a bit of horse trading, room to negotiate.

What we weren't ready for at all was what came next.

When we met with them it immediately didn't feel right. Everyone on their side's facial expressions were not positive. I don't even know why they'd bothered asking us there when they came up with what they said.

BATA's CEO and corporate accountant told us they would buy Green's from us for a pound!

Their words were something like: 'We'll buy it off you for a pound. You can walk away from it. Shall we have a bit of lunch now?'

In came the sandwiches and crisps.

Why we didn't just get up and walk away then, I have no idea. We were just stunned. F*** me, I thought. What do we do now? We sat and ate bloody sandwiches and crisps. We are stupid in this country sometimes.

We just sat there and ate lunch with these people, muted. I could not believe what had just happened. How we ate anything God knows because we were feeling very sick, very upset and to say we had had the wind taken out of our sails would be putting it mildly. We'd had our boat capsized, we'd both gone under and then someone had anchored us to the bottom of the ocean!

We had spent the best part of the last nine or ten months of our lives clinging to the hope this would go through. We'd provided them with all of the information, costing a huge amount to our business along the way.

And we were going away from this meeting with our tails between our legs and absolutely sod all! Bastards! But then again, if I was them and I had looked at all of our paperwork and finances would I have bought Green's if I was in their position? I'd probably have done exactly the same thing. Maybe.

In retrospect what happened that day in Leeds was the biggest kick up the arse financially and business-wise that I had ever had in my life.

Suddenly, after all of this, I refocused on the business. It came home to me 100 per cent that we couldn't go on the way we were.

It doesn't hurt me to admit it now, but BATA were right to offer what they had because in reality, in the clear light of day, if we hadn't done what we then did, we would have gone bust that winter and all of this would have gone. No farm. No fabulous lifestyle. No Farmer Chris.

During 2018, until October, we hadn't changed anything. Kate was more under pressure than ever. We had tens of thousands of pounds outstanding with no money to pay it all. Kate did so well to get through all of that and more without any breakdown.

Winter 2018. Christmas was coming and our Green's goose was certainly not getting fat. It was time for action.

Our profit margins we were making at the time were very low and we never saw any real profit because of the amount we had invested in stock. Our turnover was approaching £3m per year with a stocking level of approaching £500,000 and an overdraft of £200,000. Would you have bought us?

It hadn't always been this way. Our business since we had started in 2004 had grown substantially, and at first without taking on bigger overheads. But I'd done what Kate says I do. Over the years I'd become more concerned with turnover than profit, thinking that the bigger the turnover the better it would be.

We now knew it was more important to stay in business and manage it far better. We got rid of premises. We closed our Northallerton and Ruswarp branches almost immediately. We gave notice on the warehouse we were renting at Thirsk where we had been storing animal feed. We sold all the racking and sold all the feed. We didn't replace it when it had gone.

We stopped selling all livestock equipment. Cattle crushes, field gates, races, feed troughs, drinking troughs. There must have been £80,000 tied up in all that. We sold it all over three months and didn't restock that either. All of the money went straight to the bank. If farmers rang for a ring feeder we just said we didn't sell them any more.

We had a little store at Thirsk for farm products only. We gave notice on it and brought everything back into the original building that we'd started off in when we had come here.

We had a polytunnel that we'd put up outside. We took that down and Thirsk Mart built us a proper extension so that we now had a mini warehouse. I really must mention all at Thirsk and particularly Ian Woodhead who has always looked after us so well.

We didn't stop selling animal feed, we just stopped buying a 20-tonne load and instead bought a 2-tonne load every other day. Better management of supplies, less space used. With so much less space used we massively reduced our rent and our rates.

We looked at every item we sold and put prices up where we could and only stocked the lines that were profitable by the right margin. The majority of our turnover was from farming supplies and many of those you don't make a lot of money from. Many were low-margin consumables for livestock.

Anything that didn't meet that criteria we didn't stock any longer. We'd learned a hard lesson by what had happened in Leeds in October and we were fighting our way back.

We were also delivering to customers as well as having those that came into our store at Thirsk. We stopped deliveries. We told our customers that if they wanted anything from us they would have to pick it up. We went from three vans on the road to none and we sold all three vehicles.

Farm accounts traditionally took four to eight weeks to be settled and yet anything the general public bought was paid immediately, that day. When you offer terms of payment that take 28 days or up to 62 days you have an outlay. You are giving everyone an interest free loan! So we told all our farmer customers that unless they paid up their accounts with us, their account would be closed.

And yes, we made people redundant. We did all of this during the next few months following the October meeting. Of course, nobody wants to be made redundant and we didn't like making people redundant, but by thinning down the business we didn't need the same amount of people.

But it's like Alan Sugar says on *The Apprentice* on TV, when you're in business you've got to have the skin of a rhino. Business really is dog eat dog. There is very little, if any room for sentiment and by God we were within a hair's breadth of going spectacularly bust.

We knew that our turnover would drop, but at least we had money coming in and quicker than ever before, we weren't carrying too much stock, we weren't paying massive overheads and we had reduced our costs dramatically. We'd reduced our stocking level by half, our overdraft came down and our profit levels and margins had increased. Kate was finally able to pay people without worrying who she wasn't going to have to pay as a result.

Green's is still a farmers' place first and foremost and our turnover value from farmers is still quite high thanks in the main to the high value of products such as vaccines and wormers that we have retained, but our number of farm transactions is significantly less.

Where we have capitalised even more has been in the trade with the general public.

Our retail of pet foods and accessories for dogs, cats and poultry has rocketed and that's a sector that has impressive margins. Our farm shop retail side, called Mrs Pumphrey's Farm Shop, has been a little star within the business – and we sell 500 Christmas trees a year. And everything in the country store is paid for, up front!

Last Christmas 2021 was the busiest time since we have been here and it is all done now with just five staff! Who says big is beautiful!

As I write this book it is now three and a half years since that horrible day when BATA sold us up the river by not buying us. Kate and I have been seriously paddling our own canoe furiously and with purpose ever since. What we did in those first three months after the BATA fiasco brought us back from the brink.

I had realised the error of my ways. I had badly managed where we had been heading for quite a while and had finally taken my head out of my arse! No mean feat that one!

My insistence on us buying Spring View had all been part of this. We had struggled to get a mortgage on it and our bank manager Sue had shown us how it could be done, but that had put another added pressure on to Green's.

Green's is now in a fabulous position. We have doubled our profits and halved our turnover in the past three and a half years. We have now been approached by another large farm supply business and at the time of this book going to press negotiations to sell the business properly this time are well advanced and for the kind of money we perhaps dreamed of originally.

Who knows, by the time you're reading this I may be purely Farmer Chris after all, on my farm with Kate and living happily ever after!

CHAPTER 15

SHEEP

Only We Could Have White Hebrideans!

Kate and I love going to the Outer Hebrides and the island we have fallen in love with is Barra. It only has a population of just over 1000 and that suits us both just fine. Not many people, fabulous big skies, great for walking, great for our little dogs. We don't get much chance to get away these days but when we do it is Barra that we get to.

The airport is amazing. It's a beach. Flights land on Cockle Sand in between tides. It is the only airport in the world to have regular scheduled flights arrive on the sand.

The beaches, the hills and the land of Barra are all a world away from the norm and we love it. You can also get there by ferry from Oban.

It is eleven miles long and six miles wide.

Castlebay is the main hub of the island with an iconic view of the medieval Kisimul Castle located on its own small island just across from the island's capital.

With this love of the Outer Hebrides it probably wasn't surprising that we were attracted to the Hebridean sheep breed. I now love Hebs.

We had decided to give them a try after we offloaded the Kerry Hills. They couldn't have been more different to a Kerry. Half the size and totally black, but with one feature that was definitely similar, they were lively! Apparently Hebs are used to train sheepdogs because of this.

Our thought was that as the Hebridean is only a tiny,

native breed and because we only have a smallholding that we might be able to have more of these sheep that eat less than bigger sheep.

My other thought was how their lovely black faces looked so endearing with an expression that seems as though they are permanently smiling at you. They are a tiny, hardy breed that, different to some breeds, actually want to live! They don't get problems with feet or flystrike, worms or disease and they have this most wonderful mothering and milking ability.

I bought about 20 to get started with them in Autumn 2018 getting them by looking online at what was available on sellmylivestock.com and didn't have as far to travel as the Outer Hebrides, that's for sure. They came from more or less just up the road in comparison, from a guy up at Stokesley.

We put them to a Kerry Hill tup that we had retained and had our first lambs in spring 2019. But here's an incredible thing. Firstly, they are great at lambing on their own. Secondly though, I remember walking into the lambing shed one morning and this pure black Hebridean ewe had two pure white lambs sucking on it, all except they had tiny little black noses.

It was the funniest thing. I couldn't get over it, and the lambs did ever so well. The ewes lamb so easily on their own, very rarely needing any help and they are fabulous mothers. That's down to the milk they produce and within six weeks the lambs are nearly as big as them.

We had also bought a pure Hebridean tup and so we had put around 10 of the pure ewes to him and the other ten to the Kerry Hill. Across the twenty ewes they averaged one and a half lambs each. The pure Hebs will normally have just one lamb but the prolificacy of the Kerry Hill, that averages two must have had an influence through the Kerry tup.

That put us up to 50 sheep again!

Our idea was to produce hogget rather than lamb, because Hebs are very light and don't produce a lot of lamb so we thought taking them on a bit further might work, but we soon realised we didn't have the capacity to keep them that long if we were going to breed with them again the next spring. By then our numbers could have been up nearer 150 sheep!

If you're trying to work out how we would have got to that number and more it is because we would have the previous year's lambs still with us while they aged to become hoggets and we would have had the ewes that would have lambed the next season's crop. If that only comes to 80 for you then perhaps I should tell you we bought 20 more Hebs that next autumn. Oh yes, and some Shetland ewes too! There was no stopping me!

The reason why it wouldn't work that way?

Grass. They might have been little but once you get to a certain number of sheep even of a smaller size you still eventually reach overkill on grazing. It's alright saying you could rent some more grass but that then inevitably needs more fencing and if you don't fence properly these little things have a habit of getting out – and being small they can get out of the smallest of holes you wouldn't expect.

We decided to sell all of the lambs, including the two pure whites. The crossbreds that came from the Kerry Hill tup were lovely meaty lambs. We sold some locally and we sold some of the pure Hebs to others who were in the breed or who, like us, were captivated by their endearing faces. They had all gone by the autumn of 2019.

That's when I bought another 20 Heb ewes and 5 Shetlands that look so much bigger when they are in full fleece. We were back ready for tupping time again, but this time with 45 ewes. We felt that was manageable because of their easy lambing and because if there would be a problem they were light enough to deal with too.

What you notice when both the Hebs and the Shetlands have been clipped is just why they are such good mothers! It's only then that you can properly see their udders and what a magnificent sight! The udders that these lambs suckle from is like looking at a Holstein cow's bag, it's no wonder they milk so well and their lambs grow so quickly; and put to the right tup they can actually produce a lamb with a great carcase.

To me they are just an incredible little sheep that live off hardly anything, eating the roughest of grass and weeds that also helps keep the pasture tidy.

I haven't any Hebs at the moment but I will definitely have them again, maybe even later this year – and not just for the way they look. Great sheep. If you're considering having some and just want a small breed, but then want some meaty lambs, I'd definitely recommend Hebs with something like a Kerry or Border Leicester tup – and watch out for the white ones!

CHAPTER 16

WATER

The World's First Automatic Guttering Chute!

Winter 2021/22 won't go down as the coldest winter we've ever had, not at Spring View. We had some warm winter days, but when you have cattle inside you don't really want too many of them.

Ventilation is one of the key factors in keeping your cattle healthy while they are inside. You have to ensure there is plenty of air around the cattle shed otherwise there is a very real danger of your animals contracting pneumonia or other respiratory diseases.

That's what animal husbandry is all about, constantly checking on your animals' welfare, whether that is mucking out, refreshing bedding, providing feed and water, looking at their feet, checking for any lameness, watching for their well-being in any way.

You've to have your eye on the ball every day of the week and a good deal of what you have to do with your stock depends on what the weather is doing, no matter whether they are inside or out. It impacts on everything you do.

Water became a serious issue for us one winter. You honestly don't realise how much your cattle drink until you have to find another source of providing it for them when, as happened to us, our pipes froze solid.

The cattle have all got tanks of water in their pens that provide a reservoir, but once that reservoir is not able to constantly be filled back up again, on account of the frozen pipes you very quickly know how much they consume!

This particular winter was really cold. Every water pipe in the shed was frozen. We hadn't been prepared for this at all. It was yet another lesson that just landed upon us. It was a January night, one of the exceptionally harsh, cold winter nights when your fingers don't feel like they are part of your hand, they're that numb.

That night I came back from Green's and the only way I could get water to them was from our kitchen tap. But that was 100 yards away from where it needed to be and I didn't have a hose that long! In fact we didn't even have enough hosepipe to reach from the kitchen tap to the water butts I was going to fill up 10 yards from the tap!

This wasn't a question of not having thought this through, there had been nothing ever to have to think through before! But that's farming for you. There is always a new lesson to be learned. There's always a new dilemma. You've just got to roll with it and get on with doing something.

I had 40 cattle in the shed who were out of water, or if not quite out then seriously close to it. They needed sustenance and they were in need of it right now.

It was time to think and act quickly.

I brought the tractor up to the back door with the two water butts on a trailer. It would take several loads to get them enough water for through the night and into the next day and because I'd never had to bother about knowing how much they consumed I didn't know how much to put in.

But that was the least of my worries. Getting the water out from the kitchen in a suitable quantity into the butts was the first priority, otherwise it would be the carrying of small buckets all night.

Although I say it myself I was quite ingenious!

I went and found some lengths of guttering and we ran them from the tap, across the draining board and propped up on a pallet so that water was running out of our back door and into the water butt. Brilliant! Problem solved, at least for the night.

I drove the tractor down to the shed with the two now filled water butts and Kate and I decanted the water with buckets into the tanks for the cattle to drink. Several goes later and our job was done.

We had to conduct the same delivery of water each day for five days, although the following day after inventing the automatic guttering chute the night before, it was superseded by a hosepipe of the right length to reach the butts.

It was another part of our long and continuing learning curve here at Thornton on the Hill and since then we have lagged all of the pipes in the shed and now have a tap that is serviced from a pipe that comes from under the shed floor and in theory should not freeze.

I was quite pleased with myself over the water chute, but I don't think I will be going into production of it any time soon!

CHAPTER 17

CATTLE

Oh My God, What Have I Done Now?

I was so enthusiastic, so full of myself at having a farm that I wasn't going to be content until I had filled it up completely with stock. There are several problems with that kind of attitude, especially if you are not thinking things through.

One of the immediate problems was that at the time I really didn't care too much what stock was coming here. Well, obviously I did because we went into Whitebred Shorthorns and that was a very definite decision to have a pedigree rare breed herd that we would be proud of, but the only problem was that only gave me two cows at that time.

I needed more than that!

I needed lots of cattle! I needed lots of sheep. I'd bought the 50 Mules, now I wanted to fill up the farm with cattle. I had all this shed space!

I wanted every farm building we had to have the sound of pigs, sheep and cattle. I wanted life. I was a farmer!

I thought what can I do that will mean I can get up and running straight away? That's when I thought I'd buy some calves. I enjoy feeding calves, seeing them grow. I reckoned I could make some money on them, but more importantly I'd have a lot of them to deal with here and now, or at least pretty soon. I decided that was going to be my forte.

Not being very experienced in buying calves, in fact not experienced at all, as I'd never bought one, I used a dealer who bought the calves for me and duly delivered 20 of them on to the farm in January 2016. They were baby calves of 3–4 weeks old to be bucket-reared, as the term goes.

My idea was to rear them through to 6–7 months to go into what is called the store cattle trade. That would mean I wasn't taking them through to the primestock market but getting them fed well enough for what are called the finishers, beef men who know how best to take cattle through to the right weight for the beef that ends up going on to your plate.

I thought that would be my approach. I felt that if I fed them milk, gave them good hard food and maybe also turned them out to grass I could make a decent trade at Thirsk.

At Green's we sold milk powder, which you feed to calves. I could pick it up at a cheaper price than others because of this but I'd never had any experience of how much it all cost, even if you were able to buy it at a discount!

Each calf was taking at least one full bag of milk powder and around another half bag. Each bag was costing £40. Just for those 20 calves that was an additional minimum cost of £1200, and I'd bought more calves after the initial 20!

I was also too soft with them. I let them have more than they perhaps should have. My input costs were already out of control and then you start feeding them a coarse ration, a mixture of barley and molasses and, because we can't afford a bulk buy, you buy in the more expensive way, in bags.

The idea of turning them out never happened. It dawned on me that with 50 ewes already eating grass there wouldn't be enough of it, on what was only 10 acres of grassland for my calves as well.

It was an early example of me not having thought things through and just having charged ahead, and you might not think that would be too much of a problem, but grass is a lot cheaper than buying in feed and having to constantly bed them up with straw.

Lessons were coming at me thick and fast and they were to keep coming as they always have in the past seven years.

And I'd also inadvertently caused problems for a local farmer! Oh my God, what had I done?

One of the major problems in the cattle world is something called bovine TB. It is a disease that although not massively prevalent in North Yorkshire is something that any cattle man worth his salt knows that he or she must be careful over movement of livestock.

Everything like that had gone out of my head.

All I had wanted was calves. My calves had come from Lancashire. Calves from a dairy herd. I hadn't even thought about asking about whether they were from a TB1 farm, TB4 or whatever. TB is a minefield. It is a massive problem and I hadn't realised the impact it would have on me or surrounding farms by doing this.

When we first came here this farm was on TB1 status because the previous occupant had been a cattle dealer and had been buying in cattle from all over the place.

What happens with people like that is they have their stock tested for bovine TB every 12 months, one year, which is where TB1 comes from; so when we first moved here any of our cattle would have to be tested for bovine TB, because we were still down as the previous occupant as a cattle dealer.

It's all about testing regimes for bovine TB and my neighbouring farmer explained how it could impact on him. The farmer was understandably frustrated about what I had done, but fortunately left it at just pointing out that perhaps I ought to be more careful with where I brought my stock in from.

It caused me nightmares at the time. A worst-case scenario might have meant I had inadvertently brought in bovine TB and some of his cattle could have been infected and condemned to slaughter.

He would then have had his cattle movements restricted for everything else, which could mean they could go past their optimum weight when they were going to be ready for market.

I'd caused him unnecessary problems. I hadn't until then realised the enormity of calves or any cattle being brought in on a whim by someone who didn't really know all of the implications. I was, as some would say, still wet behind the ears.

Before we started at Spring View I thought I knew a bit about farming! I knew I didn't know everything, but it turns out I knew very little about the real world and now I was finding out that I knew very little, with everything I did wrong.

Fortunately, my calves didn't have bovine TB.

There is no wonder that farmers who have been farmers all their lives look warily, and in some cases wearisome, at new people coming into farming.

It takes time assimilating all of the information about what is going on in agriculture and to think you can do it on a whim, no matter whether you were born into farming over sixty years ago, is just not on, as I was finding out.

I was truly sorry for the unnecessary angst I had caused for someone who was farming properly rather than coming at it as an enthusiastic amateur, but obviously with very little professional idea.

And then my calves started coughing! And if they are coughing like mine were coughing then they were definitely not well!

And what did they have? Dear God, surely it could not get any worse!

I was paying through the nose for feed, I was giving them more milk powder because I was trying to be nice to them. I'd upset a fellow farmer, and now my calves were ill. Oh my! Doesn't do justice to how I was feeling.

It was time to make my first contact with a vet since I had become a farmer around six months ago.

All our dogs were registered with Skeldale, the veterinary practice where Alf Wight, the vet who wrote the James Herriot books that have been so successful in film and on television twice now, had worked for many years, and where the original vets on the TV series *The Yorkshire Vet*, Julian Norton and Peter Wright, were both practising.

I rang Skeldale about my calves, explaining they were ill, and a lady vet came out. It was around April time. The lady vet took their temperatures and gave me the news. My calves had pneumonia! I couldn't believe it. I thought I'd done everything right, everything by the book.

Every one of them had to be treated. I now know how those farmers you see in *All Creatures Great & Small* feel when they are confronted with this kind of bad news and all they can see is the expense.

I had the cost of the vet's visit to pay, plus a fee for each calf treatment. There's no way out of it. It all has to be done, but you can't help feeling that this is yet another expense you hadn't bargained for on top of others that have already been more costly than you'd anticipated.

I was starting to think that this venture, that I had started out full of optimism, feeling as though calf rearing was for me, something I would really enjoy, was now not going to pay very well.

I'd had additional straw bedding costs through not being able to turn them out as I'd hoped, additional feed costs because I couldn't get them out to grass because I already had sheep munching that, additional milk powder costs because I hadn't calculated how much they would drink and now additional costs to keep them alive.

It had all turned out a much bigger task than I had envisaged for a batch of calves.

CHAPTER 18

PIGS

Sow Wars – Oh! Christopher!

I do love having pigs! It goes right back to where I started at home and how I'd originally planned my life was going to be. I was probably going to be involved with pigs forever, the way in which I had set off studying at college and then taking up pig farm management positions.

It hadn't worked out that way, but then coming here had brought me back to them. We'd had the Berkshire crosses that we'd brought in at first just as weaners to grow on for pork and then we had moved on to Oxford Sandy & Blacks.

Everything I had done with the pigs had been controllable. This was one area of farming where I had real knowledge of the animals I was working with. It was a sector that, although I hadn't worked in it for many years, I knew about. It wasn't as though everything was a new lesson for me, as it sometimes appears with cattle and sheep.

I was happy with how we had settled on the farm with the pig enterprise. A few sows, regular litters, all controllable. But I'd also still harboured some ambition of maybe one day having 20 sows, and that ambition became very nearly real when I saw an advert on preloved.co.uk

Oxford Sandy & Blacks were advertised as 'free to good home'. That was even better, although I did find it slightly odd that they would be available, I wasn't about to look a gift-horse, or in this case gift-pigs, in the mouth.

I contacted the people who were letting them go. They had been keeping them in woodland near Drax and said they just couldn't cope with them any more and that they just wanted them to go to a good home.

I just saw it as the perfect opportunity to get a long way towards my goal in one go! I was excited. There were a dozen pigs to take altogether and eight of them were sows. Add that to the 3 or 4 we had on at Spring View at the time and you have a breeding herd of a dozen sows. I would be well on my way towards the 20.

Off I went with my trailer. It's just over 40 miles if you go down by the A19 and around the York ring road. This was summer 2019 and it was bloody hot. It was about 32 degrees in my car and that set my mind thinking that I would have to make a massive wallow for 'you lot' that I now had in the trailer making my way back to Thornton on the Hill.

Had I thought this through?

Not at all. But now that I had them in the trailer and I was thinking about wallows I also started thinking about what would happen when they would all farrow. Where would I put them? Eight sows, along with the sows I already had, would mean 100 piglets on the farm. They would all need feed. They would all need looking after.

Eight doesn't sound a large number, but eight sows when you have been used to just 3 or 4 is an increase to your herd of either 200 or 300 per cent. And that means 200 or 300 per cent more of everything. Costs, time and energy. When you then add what would more than likely have been an additional 80 piglets on top of your regular 20 it doesn't take long to realise you may have bitten off more than you can chew.

I told myself, 'Christopher! Christopher! What have you done this time?' when it all became clear to me.

In farming when you breed anything you have to be aware of multiplication. If your ewes, sows and cows have babies it increases the amount of stock on your farm and therefore the number of mouths that need feeding. This is all additional expense.

That's why many farmers look to sell their stock young, because they haven't the shed space capacity or field size to look after them and they can't afford to carry on feeding them. The facts of life are that everything on a farm must pay its way.

I didn't even get to the multiplication stage! I might have, but something else I had not anticipated started that put the whole idea totally out of the window.

These buggers started fighting! They started trashing the place! They started breaking out! It was like a pig battlefield and when pigs fight it can be very nasty. They don't spare the rod at all!

They were fighting with my existing sows, digging great big holes under the fence doing their own version of *The Great Escape* and generally making an absolute nuisance of themselves.

I suppose that if they'd been used to being left to it in woodland where they were probably left to their own devices they may have had much more space and so weren't used to what they had come to.

My sows were probably very wary too of new sows and a number of them all suddenly appearing. In retrospect it was bound to be unsettling for all of them. And there was I, someone who allegedly knew about pigs, in the middle of all this mayhem.

I kid you not, it was another nightmare.

Imagine the scene. I'm chasing after this bloody sow that has got away. She's going up the hill like she's the fastest sow in the world and I'm trying to catch my breath while also trying to catch her before she does some damage elsewhere or even to herself.

It was ridiculous. It was totally irresponsible of me, again, and had all been a huge mistake.

So, I sold them.

I know the people that I'd taken them away from had wanted to let them go to a good home, which they had, but it turned out only for a short while.

There was part of me that now thought there was a very good reason why these pigs had been on that website. Had I got MUG stamped on my forehead? They weren't pedigree registered either and I needed them to be, for my rare breed farm status that I was moving towards.

They needed them away because they couldn't cope with them and weren't the people to take the pigs to market. I couldn't cope with them because they were bloody crazy! But I could take them to market – and I did!

What I made from them was nearly enough to pay for the damage and havoc they had caused, to say nothing of the trauma to my existing sows – and no, there isn't a video you can watch of me chasing the sow up the hill where my cows were and landing in something decidedly soft ... and chewy! Yuk!

CHAPTER 19

COWS

Lochie Big Tits

Giving cows and bulls their names is one of the joys of cattle rearing. The old saying that people are names not numbers works the same way with cattle when you're in the breeding world.

They're usually made up of two or three words for the official herd book entries with the first word, in the case of the Whitebred Shorthorns, being the herd prefix of where the animal has been born and the second the cow or bull's name. In some cases the initial letter of this name has to be the same for each animal born in the herd that year.

But then, once that has been done, you usually settle into a nickname, which is often a shortened version of the name you've come up with.

Our first cows had been Bertha and Lochie, but Lochie was a shortened version of the cow's first name Lochdochart Snowfall and we just stuck with calling her Lochie.

When I bought another Lochdochart Snowfall, so called because it was from the same line as our first, but with a number at the end to distinguish it, from the breed's most distinguished and well-respected breeder Donald Hendry in 2019 we fondly referred to her as a quite different nickname!

Big Tits.

She had this massive udder that was nearly trailing

on the ground it was that big. She was quite an old cow, but Donald had told me to try and keep her right because she was a very old-fashioned, well-bred cow that bred immaculate calves and would really help my herd in the future.

Donald said to get as many calves off her as I possibly could. We got her in-calf and she produced a beautiful calf in 2020. Donald had been right.

Big Tits had calved alright, that was good, and we got her back in-calf okay, but about May-time of 2021 when she was going to calve for the second time while on our farm I really didn't think she looked right.

I knew she was getting ready to calve but it didn't feel right. We all pick up on body language whether it is humans or animals and I was getting really concerned because she wasn't getting on with it. I just knew there was a reason why. There had to be something that was stopping her.

I put an arm in and had a feel inside her. I thought I could feel three legs, but not a head. That was one leg more than there should be for the way in which a calf is presented for being born. I had a momentary feeling that perhaps she was having twins but really wasn't confident of anything. All I knew was we were in trouble.

There was no way I should be conducting anything further like this on my own. I called the vet.

It was early Sunday morning somewhere around 5am–6am. Big Tits was laid on her side quivering, like a sow does before she farrows, but Big Tits was a cow and she didn't look or feel right now. You could tell she was wondering what was going on and just wanted to give birth to her calf, the job she had done year-in, year-out previously without problems.

Thankfully, the vet who came was one of Bishopton vets' partners Phil Alcock and one of the most experienced

I could have had visit. He put his arm in and said that the problem was that the head was back and that he would do his best to get it presented properly.

Half an hour later he gave me the news that he couldn't get to the head to move it and that the only thing for it was to perform a Caesarean.

My heart sank. I knew this was always fraught with danger. All of this and I could lose Big Tits and her calf.

It is at moments like these when, to me, you know whether you are a proper farmer or not, someone who cares about his or her animals. Yes, farming has to be profitable among those who are relying on it for their living, but farming and particularly livestock farming is caring about your animals – and I care about mine very much.

Poor old Big Tits was going through hell and in a short time would be going through far more than males of any species ever have to go through. Ladies, I salute you wherever you are!

This was the first time we would ever have had a C-section on a cow at Spring View. I suppose you could say we had caught lucky in not having had to go through one in our first three years.

The vet apologised, not that he had to because it wasn't his fault, but said there was no other real option. He said the only other thing was to carry on with what he was trying to do in manipulating the calf but that he could feel the calf was alive and that he would rather get it out alive by C-section. The danger would be if he left it too long it would die inside.

Big Tits was an old cow and didn't want to get up. I think she was knackered from the stress of having this calf inside, that by now should have been out and sucking on the teats of her impressive bag.

The vet left her laid on her side and began shaving

her to put all of the antiseptic on while he was waiting for another vet to arrive as they had to have two of them.

I was transfixed as they went about conducting the operation. I watched everything, how they had to move the rumen out of the way, how they had to hold parts of this dear old cow. It was really interesting and you really do understand why being a doctor or a vet is such a demanding profession.

They got to the calf and because it was quite big they asked if I would get hold of its legs and gently pull it out.

One of the vets was holding Big Tits' guts in while the other held the uterus and I'm pulling this calf out ever so gently.

It was quite an incredible thing to see and play my part in. It was a bull calf and I immediately had his name – Caesar!

The vets stitched up Big Tits and what a superb job they did of everything. It had been three and a half hours since the first vet had arrived and we now had a live cow and a live calf.

But there's always something. Big Tits wouldn't get up and that meant Caesar couldn't suckle. Oh my!

Kate came to the rescue. She milked quite a lot of milk from Big Tits' massive udder and gave Caesar his colostrum. All's well that ends well? Hmm. As it turned out, kind of no, at first. The cow still wouldn't get up.

Now I know what you ladies are probably thinking, she was knackered, she's just had an emergency operation performed on her, she'd had this mighty big calf brought out a way she had never experienced, she'd been cut open and now she had been stitched up and probably didn't know what the hell had just happened. Who wouldn't want to just lie there and try to get some kind of rest?

But by about 7 o'clock that night her restorative powers must have been coming back because she was up in her pen and we got Caesar sucking on her. He must have thought all his Christmases had come at once when he saw the size of them! Or was that just me?

She looked fully recovered, back to her normal self and her stitches were looking great when three days later I came home from Green's and there she was laid on her side again. She was in the field now and quivering again. Caesar was next to her.

I thought maybe she had gone down with calcium deficiency, milk fever? But of course I had no real idea.

I called for the vet again. He gave her everything he could from a magnesium injection to drenches and still she wouldn't get up.

Eventually, after the vet had done all he could for her, I thought that maybe I could coax her up. She wasn't responding to anything but she was still alive.

I put a bale of straw on the front of my tractor, something that I thought if I drove carefully enough would push her gently and that might just make her get up if she could. It did the trick, but only partially. She ended up sat like a dog and we put the bale of straw alongside her, but she died overnight with her lovely calf alongside her. I'd kind of expected it, but it was, as it always is when you lose an animal, so sad.

It was such a sad ending to what had been such a joyous moment when Caesar had been brought out from her, but maybe she had never fully recovered, maybe it had all just been too much for the old girl.

We did what you have to do in those circumstances to make sure Big Tits went on her way off the farm, but new life needs looking after and we had a three-day-old calf that had lost its mum.

Bless him, he was trying to suckle off her when she was long since gone. And we still needed to make sure he got everything he needed. Kate fed him on the bottle, we brought him over to the shed where he was near some other calves for company and Caesar is now a lovely, impressive young bull.

You think what you should have done to keep any animal alive. You always reproach yourself a little, sometimes a lot, for not noticing some sign days, weeks and perhaps months ago, but this hadn't been down to anything I'd done.

I'd had a top vet from Bishopton Vets, who are really, truly marvellous. The caesarean had been performed extremely well. In the end, in farming, there is a well-known phrase that I've said once in this book and will say it again – where you have livestock there is always going to be deadstock. Big Tits had served her time. She'd been a grand old cow, but time catches up with all animals and us too!

If we hadn't done what had been done to get Caesar out she would most likely have died anyway, with him inside her.

I still smile when I think of her name though!

CHAPTER 20

BULLS

Wow! It's George William!

I'm a father and I have two wonderful sons Rob and David. I'm very proud of them and what they have achieved in their lives.

As a farmer and pedigree cattle breeder I am also proud of what we have been responsible for breeding and that was brought home to me even more one day at the autumn show and sale of Whitebred Shorthorns at Borderway Mart in Carlisle in 2021.

Lochie and Bertha had both produced bull calves as our first homebred stock in 2016. I'd been disappointed at the time. When you are keen to push on with expanding your herd you want your cows to produce heifers, so that you have your own homebred cows in the herd without buying in from other farms.

We had bought Elizabeth in-calf in November 2016, the pedigree cow we had seen at the Great Yorkshire Show that had brought about our love of Whitebred Shorthorns in 2015. And it was Elizabeth who produced our first home-born heifer calf Lady Kathryn in March 2017.

Bertha brought about our second heifer calf to be born at Spring View in June 2017 when Tabitha was the result of having put Bertha with top Whitebred Shorthorn bull Ben Ledi Joe.

Lochie produced another bull calf. We'd put Lochie to AI, which was something I had wanted to try because of bloodlines, bringing in new ones to the herd. We had used it on Bertha, but she didn't hold and that's why she ended up having Tabitha in June as she was now out of synch.

One of the things I want to do when I have the time is to train in AI as an official inseminator, because the problem with AI-ing cattle is that when you are not qualified you have to use others such as Genus who might only be able to arrive at certain times and you need to be able to make sure the inseminator is here at the right time for when the cows are at the right stage to AI.

But Lochie's AI had held and she produced our bull calf George William. I called him after my father and I really quite liked him, but you can only run so many bulls and when you only have what was then a very small herd it is limited on which cows he could be used on, and that meant certainly not his mother Lochie!

We had reared him ourselves and had sold him as a yearling bull at the Carlisle sale at 15 months. We hadn't seen him since that time, but he had been working for three years when we next saw him, back at Carlisle in autumn 2021.

I'll let Kate tell part of this story, because she'd been aware of George William coming to Carlisle again.

"It was quite funny the way it worked out. I'd read my catalogue beforehand and I knew that George William was going to be there. I'd told Chris. As we were getting our cattle ready to get into the pens all these cattle came down the right-hand side and there was a Whitebred bull. He was huge. My first thought was that this couldn't be George William, but once we had got our six penned up I checked his ear tag.

"I thought I would try Chris out a little and just said, 'What do you think to this bull then?' and he said, 'That's a good bull.' When I said it was George William, Chris couldn't believe it."

I really couldn't. I'd known that George William was a good bull, but what I saw now, three years on, was this magnificent animal. So big, long and such a nice shape. I just wish I could have bought him. He is a superb specimen of a Whitebred Shorthorn, and he sold for 2200 guineas!

What a great feeling it was for us too. One of our homebred animals looking so well and obviously performing well. The auctioneer said some fantastic words before he sold him. He said something like this: 'The Jefferys from Spring View Farm bred this beautiful animal. They had their own cattle here earlier today.'

I don't think either of us could have been more pleased. Chuffed to having had our herd prefix mentioned among the other Whitebred breeders and very proud of what we had produced from our little farm.

There is nothing more satisfying in farming than seeing that what you have produced is appreciated by other breeders and other cattle men and women.

Who knew that when I was initially disappointed when my cows were having bull calves that just a few years later I would end up being so proud of one that we had reared.

There are so many stories that end with the heartache of animals that reach an emotional climax to their lives, but this was a story that offered me real pride in what Kate and I are trying to do.

Watching George William in the ring was just like watching my boys years ago.

CHAPTER 21

TRACTORS

My First Tractor

My granddad never had a tractor. He farmed with heavy horses, his two Shires Tommy and Laddie. Granddad always wore a collar and tie, waistcoat, jacket, corduroy trousers and a hat while he was out in the fields as many did from his generation.

I'd driven tractors when I'd worked on farms but I'd never had one of my own until we moved to Spring View when I got my first one, a Deutz Fahr. It was another special moment to get into the cab of my own tractor on my own farm.

I'd got it from my very good friend Tim Robson who doesn't live very far away from us and has his own farm and his own farm machinery business. I got a loader from him also. When you've a livestock farm that's one of the most essential things.

Your tractor is the workhorse that would have been the actual workhorses that my granddad had. And there was stacks of work to do that involved me hauling or carrying stuff all around our farm. At least with a loader you can lift things up and move things around easier, likes bales of straw and hay.

I'd had a small tractor at Scriven House Farm when I'd been in my teens, but this was different. This was mine, a proper tractor, four-wheel drive and green!

Most people think of John Deere when they think of

a green tractor but Deutz Fahr is a well-respected brand manufactured in Germany. It was perfect for me when I was setting up.

This tractor has been the love of my life, a lovely old girl. I bought her second-hand, but more recently she's not been herself.

It all started when I was driving her home down our little country lane one day. I was driving up the hill a good mile away from home when her steering went! Oh my!

I can turn the steering wheel but the tractor's wheels are not moving in response. Fortunately, the fault appears intermittent which allows me the opportunity to somewhat miraculously get back home. I am working out what I need to do in order to get back. I have a right hand, left hand and then another right hand to make with a trailer on the back carrying bits of gates and fencing.

I am seriously stressed. I am just trying my best to hold a straight line, talking to myself. I have to get through our closest village of Oulston and then negotiate a tricky right turn on to my little country lane back to our little hamlet of Thornton on the Hill.

I have memories of my previous tractor incident when I was driving home with a cattle feed ring that fell off the back of my trailer, and for a second it flashes through my mind that the white van man who saw my cattle ring bounding in his direction then will appear out of nowhere and not believe it is the same farmer!

I still have my brakes, it's only the steering that's the problem, and I've not lost some heavy farm kit irresponsibly. I could just stop. But then I'm in the way, and anyway, I just want to get back and then worry about what to do and the expense it will cost to get it back right.

I go as slowly as I can around the corners, the bends, spinning the steering wheel as much as I can to coax the tractor's wheels into turning enough to keep me on the road. Miraculously, I manage to turn a little and somehow get back with no harm to anyone, apart from my stress level!

This happened in October 2021 and in March 2022, £2000 lighter and a new hydraulic pump later, my old girl is as good.

People who are involved in farming always help each other, that's something I've really learned since we moved here and I've been very lucky that my friend and local straw dealer Richard Greenwood has helped me out with jobs on the farm with his Kramer telescopic handler that he keeps here.

Richard lives in the village and comes to see what needs doing and helps me fill the silage rings and put the straw in, but he may have seen my previous escapades with my tractor because he doesn't trust me anywhere near his Kramer!

I am ever so grateful for what Richard does and without him I would have been stuffed. While I knew a tractor was useful I really didn't realise just how important my tractor was until I couldn't use it, and as I write this it is coming to the time of year when I need to put on tillage and spray thistles, which can't be done with a Kramer.

We have land that is three miles away from the farm and you really need a tractor over there to do the jobs that need doing. I know a lot of people talk about things like telescopic handlers, materials handlers and quad bikes for getting a lot of work done around a farm but I really need a tractor.

Whether I'm loading a trailer on the back with equipment that is needed or stuff that is to come back from a field, or for fertiliser spreading, topping or harrowing, it's my tractor that works best for me.

CHAPTER 22

FARMER KATE

We Have to Make This Work

This is not about me, it's about my wonderful wife, who I love dearly and if it wasn't for Kate we wouldn't be at Spring View Farm and I wouldn't have become the farmer I always wanted to be.

Here's Farmer Kate to tell you a bit about herself. You've heard me mention her a great deal, now it's time for Kate:

I was born in Ripon Maternity Hospital in 1957, daughter to my parents Len and Heather Dickinson. My dad farmed at Marton-cum-Grafton near Boroughbridge in North Yorkshire where he had pigs, calves and beef cattle as well as milking around a dozen cows.

I have always loved horses and ponies and had my first pony, Sweep, when I was 4 years old. Dad bought Sweep from Otley market as a two-year-old and from that moment on I have always ridden. I ride out as much as I can, pretty much daily around Spring View and on the country lanes and across the fields.

One of my fondest memories growing up was when John Swan, who used to work for my dad at Marton, used to come to work on his horse. I used to run up the road to meet him at Wood Corner, I must have been about 5 or 6 years old, and he'd put me on the front of his saddle and we'd ride the rest of the way together.

I was 9 years old when we moved over to Brompton-by-Sawdon, going towards Scarborough, when Mum and Dad bought Sawdon Heights in 1967.

It was a very big move at the time because Dad had previously rented a council farm at Marton, but now had his own place and a much bigger farm as it ran to 170 acres. The farm was made up of arable land, cattle, pigs and, of course, ponies!

I'd do anything on the farm, like most farmers' kids at that time. I'd help rear the calves, make sure they were fed, had fresh bedding, mucked out; I'd lamb the sheep; and I'd usually be the one responsible for milking the house cow for our own milk. We had a Jersey cow for many years and later we also had a Whitebred Shorthorn. So, my life has come full circle.

Dad had a commercial flock of Mule ewes and he used to go to Cheshire to buy crossbred commercial calves to bucket-rear. He went into partnership running a pig unit on the farm with another local man, Brian Thomas from Sawdon who designed specialist pig buildings.

I went into pedigree sheep in my 20s with my dad. We went into Bleu du Maine from France, which was a relatively newly imported breed at the time in the early 80s because we quite liked the look of them and we both saw it as an upcoming breed with real potential. We bought them between us.

I enjoyed showing, as well as being with the other girls and having a great time. We all enjoyed both of those things. There would be myself, Christine Thompson, Marilyn Tate, Elaine Keith and Tina Blyth. We had such a good time and were sometimes slightly worse for wear the next day.

My job was to get everyone back right. We'd get to Harrogate for the Great Yorkshire Show on a Sunday, even though the show didn't start until Tuesday. That meant we could really enjoy ourselves on the Sunday night and spend Monday recovering. Sunday night was always the best night. I can never forget helping Christine recover the next morning one time.

We would get to all of the local shows and some of the big ones too – the Great Yorkshire, Lincolnshire, Notts & Newark, Ryedale, Thornton-le-Dale, Driffield, Pateley (Nidderdale), Malton, and further south Three Counties Show at Malvern where I got reserve champion with a gimmer shearling I'd bred myself. I won a class at the Great Yorkshire with a tup that I'd bought from John Page who farmed at Penrith.

We moved on from showing Bleu du Maine sheep to Suffolks after having become friends with Alan Upton who was Raymond Twiddle's shepherd and I had a winner at Malton with a ram lamb I'd bred. I was very proud of that.

I'm looking forward to showing our new Border Leicester flock at one or two shows this year, maybe the Great Yorkshire Show and Ryedale Show. It depends on how we get on with everything. It will be my first time in years.

Horses have always played a massive part in my life. I became a member of the Derwent Hunt Pony Club and have hunted, evented, been involved in pony club games, team chases and point to point all through the Derwent. And I've driven too, winning in the FEI single horse class at Lowther Park in 1981! That's what HRH Prince Philip used to do.

We used to go down to Badminton Horse Trials every other year where we became good friends of Brian Higham who was stud groom there for 50 years. I remember the first time we went was with a friend because they had a runner there. We were staying in a caravan and Dad came back saying he couldn't believe that he'd just met someone he used to go to school with. It was Brian, who was a Yorkshireman too. After that we went often and I would go for a week at a time and spend time with Brian as a groom.

My first experience of hunting was when I was 10 years old. I hunted with Dad who had an Arab X Welsh Cob called Symphony. I went from Sweep to Llani to a cob called Ben, to Edward and rode in Point-to-Point races, once coming second in the Farmer's Race at Charm Park.

One of the things I'd wanted to do with a horse was to train and ride my own pointer. I bought Edward, whose proper name was Burnt Heath, who I'd bought from Thomas Harrison, my friend Fiona's husband. Fiona and I had grown up together. She had come down from Scotland when she was 16 and we have been good friends ever since. Edward was a thoroughbred, standing at 15.3 hands and just the right size for me. I evented with him too.

I do love farming. It's something I grew up with and I do like lambing sheep, calving cows and looking after them, but maybe I didn't have quite the burning passion that Chris had when we started.

I'm the one that bottle-feeds either the calves, the piglets or the lambs if they need it. As this book was being completed I've all three triplets from one ewe that I'm bottle-feeding to top them up and I'll be involved with the ewe that's having quads. I'll bottle-feed anything to give our animals the best chance.

When Chris has been away filming it is sometimes tricky being on the farm on my own. I recall our Whitebred Tabitha had calved a heifer calf that became Springview Heather and Tabitha was maybe just on the young side to have her because she hadn't got enough milk. We'd had to get the vet out to calve her.

Heather was only a little thing when she was born. I'd kept looking at Heather because I just felt she wasn't coming on just right. She wasn't getting enough milk. So I decided I must feed her, but I was on my own and Tabitha was a bit flighty. The first time I tried it took me about three-quarters of an hour to get Heather in the shed, but once she knew why she was coming she would then come to me every day. I fed her all summer. It got to the stage where I would just take a bottle up the field each night and feed her. She turned into a really nice heifer.

But horses are my thing. I love my horse Lorna and to have my own farm where I can do all the riding out that I want is great. I also know riding is good for me. It's what I love doing and where we live is just perfect. I'm good at opening and shutting gates too!

What I know is that farming doesn't make lots of money, so for me, to live here we have to make money and that's why Green's has always come first. I'm the banker, and to make my life easier I have to see lots of money coming in.

I shall do my best to help Chris make the farm a success, which probably at best means just making it viable. I'm not saying I will be successful, but I'll do my best to make it pay.

There won't be any masterplan of saying we have to do this much by this time or other. It will be like we've done with Green's. It will evolve.

CHAPTER 23

COWS

My God! It's the Biggest Calf We've Ever Had!

In November 2017 we bought an in-calf heifer called Northwood Katherine, another from Helen Chard's prefix. She's quite a big cow and she started to calve again in July last year. It was a lovely summer's evening about 7 o'clock when she started.

She'd had a history of having her calves really quickly, just popping them out, but this time she'd been in labour for getting on for three hours. I thought I'd have a go at trying to help her but after having put my arm in I said to Kate that I didn't think we could get it out.

It was another call to the vet as I thought that if we didn't we were going to lose something, either the cow, the calf or both. It was about 10 o'clock when I rang and said Katherine was struggling and I'd tried but I needed someone to come. I was told a vet would be with me within the hour.

But Katherine was really giving it her best shot. She was lying down and pushing and straining as hard as she could. Time was running out. This calf was on its way, but it wasn't coming out. There was something wrong. And the vet hadn't arrived as yet.

To be fair it was still within the hour of when we knew she was due to arrive, but that wouldn't be any consolation to Katherine and her calf.

We had to do something!

I said to Kate that we were going to have to do what we could between us.

Previously I'd had a vet to the farm who had calved a cow for us using our calving jack and I remembered how he had done it, with me helping. That meant I knew how Kate and I could do it together.

We got this calving jack on and I took the vet's role and told Kate what I needed her to do, to work the jack while the calf was coming while I held the calf.

I'd only used this jack once before and so we were both very inexperienced but like I said that doesn't matter to Katherine, she's just trying to give birth to her calf.

I got the ropes on to the calf's ankles and we started to jack. I was telling Kate the same thing that the vet had told me, to move the jack up and down, while I was pulling and pulling and its head was starting to come out. With one big tug and a pull, a lot of sweating and swearing we got the calf out successfully.

Oh my God!

There was no wonder this calf was so difficult for Katherine to calve. It was the biggest Whitebred Shorthorn we had ever had born. It was massive. It was getting towards 11 o'clock at night and both Kate and I are lying there in the shit and the muck and the blood and the blather, and this cow now gets up and comes and licks its calf, enough to say, What the f*** are you two doing here? I've got my calf, now piss off.

We just looked at each other and smiled. We'd done it. I had birthing fluid all over me, but I couldn't have cared less. There is nothing as wonderful as seeing new-born animals and especially for us a new-born calf, which on this occasion we'd not just bred but had also helped birth it.

What an achievement for us both!

There are times when things go wrong on a farm, there

are times when you can't control things. But when they go right and you have controlled, or at very least helped, it is the most amazing feeling. It made us feel so good that night. It needed us both. That's the other thing.

Kate and I really worked so hard to prise this huge calf out gently and slowly. It is so important not to over stress the cow in this kind of situation where she is obviously going to be stressed.

Fortunately for myself and Kate we were doing this with a good, experienced cow – and we had another fantastic bull calf, Springview Lord William.

CHAPTER 24

PIGS

Penny Pig

The one thing Kate has never really been as involved with is the pigs and it tickled me when she asked when seeing a sow having a litter, in all innocence, 'Doesn't the sow turn around to lick its piglets?'

If it is a ewe or a cow that has just given birth the mother gets around and licks it dry, but pigs are different. The sows don't need to do this at all because all the piglets do is come out and go straight on to the udder on one of the sow's many teats.

But Kate had the last laugh on me a little while later, which served as a very real reminder that you can have been around pigs or any animal nearly all your life, or certainly for a long period of time, and still be shown something new.

We had this sow called Smiler who was a very prolific sow. She had a massive litter of 16 piglets and there was no way she could feed them all. Because there were so many you usually get some small ones and they need to feed quickly to have any real chance of surviving, let alone stay out of the way of being rolled on and squashed by the sow.

Kate decided she was going to help the tiniest of them all from Smiler's litter and went to get a lamb feeding bottle. In all the years I've kept pigs I have never seen anybody feed a baby pig with one and I said it would never work. How wrong was I?

That little pig, just like my favourite little Hebridean sheep, definitely wanted to live and took to the bottle. Kate called it Penny Pig. And then she proceeded to feed some of the other smaller ones too.

There they all were, sucking on this bottle like new-born lambs. Kate said she only did it because she really had to, but that Penny Pig had become her favourite. It just showed me that you never stop learning on a farm. There's always something that can make you happy or sad, up or down, and sometimes the most amazing things happen and sometimes something really unexpected. Kate certainly taught me a new lesson that day.

Penny Pig then gave us a bit of a scare a bit later. We turned the piglets outside with their mother Smiler. Kate, who was now watching over Penny as her pet pig, said she didn't think Penny was looking very well. Kate brought her back inside, she fed her again and put her in a basket to keep her warm.

Kate loved Penny Pig and the story became even better. Not only did Penny Pig survive, we kept her as a breeding gilt.

Penny Pig had a litter of 8 piglets, but then her life took a final twist when she suffered an anal prolapse. It was out so much that we chose to not let her suffer any longer.

Kate was so upset. Penny was her pet pig – and she just said to 'Get Cooper' our neighbour and licensed slaughterman. It was a sad end for Penny Pig.

CHAPTER 25

GRASS

Grass Is a Crop & Moles Are a Menace

When we first came here in 2015, we took on 10 acres of grassland. Seven years on and with rented land we now have 40 acres. It's all grass. We don't grow anything else, no crops like cereals or root crops like potatoes or carrots, although some of the land we have now acquired has grown potatoes in the past. I need the grass for my animals to graze.

I remember my old lecturer Brian Thomas (not the pig building man of the same name) at Askham Bryan College used to drill it in to all of us that GRASS IS A CROP, DON'T FORGET THAT! And now that I have 40 acres of the stuff and keep cattle and sheep that live off it, it is up to me to ensure I make the most of it.

Grass is seriously important to every livestock farmer and grassland management is something that we all try to get right. It is a really cost effective way of providing your cattle and sheep with nutrition.

You don't just use it to graze your animals either, many farmers also cut it to make silage or hay or haylage for feeding your livestock through the winter when they can't graze. We don't at present because we haven't enough land to devote to it.

I need as much grass to grow as quickly as possible to feed my animals during summer, and I also want it to be the best quality grass it can be.

In October 2021 I totally rotavated the newly acquired land that had had potatoes in it previously, leaving the soil in a smooth condition. We then drove over with a tillage spinner. We put grass seed into the spinner to broadcast it across the field and went over it with a roller. It has taken nicely.

I'm always very keen to get the sward established quickly and each year, as soon as the weather is dry and warm enough, apply the right fertiliser. Sometimes if the land has warmed up sufficiently as it did a few years ago you can apply fertiliser as early as February. It is all worked out on the average daily temperature from January 1 and usually that comes down to around mid-March application.

It's also about knowing what to put on your land. My old pastures need potassium and phosphorous as well as nitrogen, but the new ley will want more nitrogen to get it going.

Unfortunately, in recent times the cost of doing just that has tripled and even getting the right nitrogen was going to be difficult this year as I write this.

If I had been able to get the new ley established in spring 2021 it would have worked out better cost wise because the fertiliser price had gone through the roof at that time, but that is farming. I couldn't because of the weather conditions. It had been the coldest, driest spring on record but then it had been followed by the wettest May. If I had planted seed in that field last spring it wouldn't have taken.

My cattle would be far happier and healthier outside all winter, as the sheep are apart from lambing time, but they would destroy the grassland. Come springtime there would be all mud and no grass.

And one thing you must not do with a newly established ley is to turn the cattle out on it at the start, because the first thing that happens to cattle whenever they are turned out after being in a building for the winter is they go bananas!

They run around like absolute idiots and can easily destroy all of the good work you have done, wrecking the root mass in the soil.

That's why it's sheep that will be allowed on first and for the whole of winter.

Pest control is another important part of farming and moles in fields are a menace. You might not think the odd molehill makes a lot of difference, but if you have molehills in your pasture they can create an awful mess. Although we don't make silage ourselves, silage with soil in it can be contaminated by mole activity and cause disease in livestock.

We harrow the grass in springtime so that we knock down as many molehills and so that new grass can come through. We also control the weeds too, otherwise you can soon find you are losing a significant proportion of your effective grassland.

We've had problems with moles, but that's where our 'whack-a-mole' champ comes in – Richard the Molecatcher – and no, he doesn't use his Kramer on them!

CHAPTER 26

SHEEP

Border Leicesters

We've had quite a journey with our sheep at Spring View in the relatively short time we've been here. Our learning curve has involved where we've wanted to go, what breed we have really wanted to keep and what breed really suits us and the farmland we have.

The Kerry Hills were fabulous to look at, but for us had proved a bit difficult to manage. The Hebrideans I'd loved, and we will go back to shortly. The Shetlands were good too. We'd always fancied Herdwicks because they look so different and had had five or six of those at the same time as we had the Hebs and the Shetlands.

The problem with us then having three separate pedigree flocks is that you need a pedigree tup for each breed and you need to ensure you keep them all separately otherwise they will destroy each other.

We had bought the Herdwicks from a local farmer, Richard Bell from Sutton Bank, as I'd felt there was a market for Herdwick females. This had come to me because when we looked for ewes we had struggled. My business brain had kicked in with the old supply-and-demand concept that if we had ewes and a tup we could breed females for others.

What I'd not thought through quite properly was the time this would take because you don't normally start selling ewes for breeding until they are at least a year old, which would mean increasing numbers of sheep on the farm again, as then I would have at least two years' worth of lambing still here.

I would then need more room to keep them, especially with flocks of Hebrideans and Shetlands too.

It wasn't as though we had that many ewes overall, around 40 at the time, but with three separate breeds and trying to ensure the tups were all kept apart and not jumping over into the other fields it was going to be a logistical nightmare. Something was bound to go wrong!

We tried. We had the Herdwick tup and females on one part of the farm, but with the fencing we then had to put up to enclose them, plus the other breeds, plus providing enough grazing for the cattle, we discovered we hadn't enough grass.

We persevered for a year but finally discovered that it wasn't going to work – and this was where the Border Leicesters came in.

The Border Leicester breed started out with the famous Robert Bakewell's Dishley Leicester flock being involved in a breeding programme that saw it crossed with Teeswaters and Cheviots to become what was then known as the Redleg in the 18th century and becoming the Border Leicester in 1850.

Its ability to produce Mule sheep by being crossed with a hill breed means that it has a commercial place. Its ewes' best traits are its mothering ability that produces fast-growing, early maturing lambs. To my mind it hit two marks. It was a good pure bred pedigree animal and also a highly efficient crossing sire. The sheep equivalent of our Whitebred Shorthorns.

I'd read that the Border Leicester crossed with the Hebrideans produces lovely Mules, and that it did the same with Herdwicks.

Most Border Leicester breeders are based in

Northumberland and, perhaps unsurprisingly, the Border Counties. Kate and I visited a breeder in Northumberland where I'd found this young, beautiful pedigree registered Border Leicester tup called Peter.

We had a really nice day and the people who sold him to us knew me as Farmer Chris from the telly! As we were leaving with Peter, they said to make sure he gets on telly next time you're on!

We put him on to some of our Hebrideans and right enough they did produce some really cracking, lovely lambs. We sold a few in the back end of last year at Thirsk as store lambs and they did really well, showing the potential of the Border Leicester as a crossing breed.

Peter had been put on to these tiny black Hebs and they had all produced white lambs with a nice tight fleece. We had creep-fed them concentrated pellet feed, had taken 15 to market and had made very good prices for 25–35 kilos.

In the market they were sold as continentals because they were white and how good they looked, which was similar to Thirsk's commercial stock that goes through every week. Who would have thought that would be the case from little black sheep?

If they had been little black things it would have been a completely different story.

That's when Kate and I got to thinking that these beautiful Border Leicesters are some really smart sheep, in appearance and what they can do. We'd already been taken with their big, erect ears and people were walking by the farm on our country lane and asking what breed they were. They really are a stunning breed, highly attractive, pleasing on the eye – but now they were something more to us.

Having had various breeds of sheep we now decided it was time to have a focused plan. And what that brought about was the sale of all breeds we had on the farm at the time and to buy Border Leicesters. We were now moving into a breed in the similar way we had with the Whitebreds.

And we got off to a bad start! Well, who would have guessed!

I bought our first two ewes from Emma Barron in Malton. One went lame. She had a problem with her hip. We persevered with her but she didn't get in-lamb. It was as bad as this. My vet said: "Chris, you've two options. You either keep her lame because she isn't going to get any better or you shoot her."

I rang Emma, who was shocked and was very apologetic that we'd had problems and she took her back.

We then started in earnest building up our start-up flock. We got in touch with the Society of Border Leicester Sheep Breeders to find out where we could buy good quality breeding stock and the main part of the initial stock came from leading respected breeder Rob Grinnall from the Clay Farm Partnership near Worcester.

We went down to him twice buying two lots of breeding stock and since then our new tup Quartermaster, whose genetics like the rest of the flock are really good. He has also been used for AI.

We felt that those sheep, plus our scouring the country for other very good Border Leicester ewes, that took us to counties such as Herefordshire and Shropshire, should form the basis for what we were intending to be the highest quality genetic flock in the country.

The ewes we bought had only been with us a week when disaster was to strike once again.

I was out in the field and there was one missing. Couldn't find her at all. Where the hell had she got to? These aren't the wild types we'd had before, much more placid. We'd felt we could cope with them. She couldn't have escaped somehow, could she? Our fencing is pretty secure.

Where was she?

Laid dead. Riggwelted. That's when a ewe gets stuck on its back and can't get up without some form of assistance. This ewe hadn't had any. She'd been wandering about the hill, had fallen into a rigg, had riggwelted and was dead as a nit. She was to go to our new tup and so wasn't in-lamb.

All of these other breeds of sheep we'd had since we started here and we'd never lost one, at least not a supposedly healthy breeding ewe. We'd certainly never lost one like that.

We sold Peter in summer 2021 as we were upping our game now and we didn't feel he was going to be good enough for the quality of ewes we intended to have. That is, if any of them survived! At the rate we were going, losing two out of eight even before tupping, our new tup would have little to work with.

We'd bought our magnificent new Border Leicester tup Quartermaster in the summer and we put him to our ewes in September.

When we had the ewes scanned in January this year (2022) I couldn't believe it! Two of the ewes were geld! That meant they were not in-lamb, not carrying lambs. I'd bought these ewes from top pedigree breeders hoping for fabulous lambs. I'd been wanting to start off our pedigree flock with a really good gene pool of young sheep and this was a living nightmare!

I'd had one go lame, one dead and two that weren't in lamb. Not a good strike rate from a relatively small number of allegedly very good breeding ewes that had all commanded a good price. This was an absolute disaster! All dead money, as well as one dead sheep!

I tried to console myself that we'd just had a bad start and, as they say, it happens.

Looking back, we probably made a mistake in trying to synchronise the ewes so that they all came into season together. Quartermaster is a fantastic boy, but the problem was that the ewes didn't come into season as quickly as we'd hoped.

My thought had been that we should try to get our Border Leicester ewes lambing in January, as many other pedigree breeders will, so that the lambs you have look that much bigger than those born in April when you attend the summer agricultural shows and the breed society shows and sales. We'd never done it before. What could possibly go wrong?

It would mean that if it worked out okay we might be able to show some of our pedigree stock at shows this year, but it didn't really work. And it didn't really work because we hadn't done it at all properly. I'd not thought it through!

What you should do if you're going to go that way is to use sponges or hormone injections to help ewes come into season early. We didn't know much about all that and just chucked Quartermaster in in September. It was not at all the right thing to do.

Sheep are seasonal breeders and they come into heat naturally when the shortening of daylight hours bring it on.

Here we were, relative newcomers to the breed and we were instantly trying something that was unnatural to sheep; we were trying something that even a more experienced breeder would have been careful with; and we had animals that had only just arrived on the farm, that hadn't even had chance to settle before we had put something unnatural to them. Who the hell did I think I was? What was I playing at? Yes, I knew what I was trying to achieve, but there is such a thing as taking one step at a time!

I still had and have a lot to learn.

And another thing. I don't really like the idea of using

chemicals to try and alter a sheep's breeding pattern, so we're unlikely to try it this September, but we may try something that we have used before to at least get the ewes to lamb a little earlier than April.

We have used a vasectomised tup previously on the Hebs and ran him with the ewes before we put the tup in. We found it really helps bring the girls into season having a tup running with them. It's a more natural way of starting them off.

It was a Manx Loaghtan tup we'd used previously that we'd bought from Judith Hawkhead of Raskelf, but not from renowned breeder Lyn Arrowsmith who lives in the same village and has her wonderful rare-breed, award-winning animals. But for some reason we had sold Manxy thinking we wouldn't need him with such a small flock. How wrong we had been.

He might not have done the trick so early on as September, but he may have started our ewes off maybe a few weeks before November.

With what we had tried in September I think we unsettled our ewes, or maybe they had all been treated with something in the past to get them into season early and we hadn't, which again would have been unsettling.

Quartermaster still did his best, but it took us three cycles to get them all mated, only to find out two were bloody geld!

So, after the geld ewe experience, to say nothing of the dead ewe experience or the lame ewe experience, was I deterred? Not a bit of it.

Up Kate and I went to the in-lamb ewe sale of Border Leicesters at Carlisle. I took the trailer in anticipation. I thought I've only got a few, maybe I'll come home with a few more, but I sat there stunned.

It was an amazing, almost out-of-body experience.

I'd thought I might have to go to 500 to 600 guineas to

pick something up. And that was what I thought would be the highest price. Oh no. As these sheep are coming into the ring they are starting at 500 to 600 guineas.

I sat there absolutely gobsmacked.

On average the in-lamb ewes made between 1500-2000 guineas that day. The record price was made for a ewe lamb not even a year old. It made 3000 guineas.

I managed to pinch one, not a very good looking one, for 550 guineas, and I bought another two ewe lambs right at the end of the sale for 600 and 700 guineas.

Kate was alongside me with the catalogue, writing down how much they were all making and who had bought them, and she said, 'Who bought that last one?'

I coughed and said, 'I did.' Kate just looked at me, in that way, and said, 'What!?'

My justification was that I'd thought I couldn't just buy one ewe lamb and I'd already bought the one at 600 guineas and there was only this one left. Just before the sale I'd been talking to the breeder from Herefordshire who was selling them. This last one had got to 650, someone had gone in at 670 and the auctioneer came back to me at 700. It was all over in a flash.

We were bringing back home one in-lamb ewe carrying a single lamb and two ewe lambs. Three and perhaps four more to breed from in 2023.

But this sale had woken me up to the breed's potential. Kate and I both now realised the value of our breed. I was excited. We have these breeding sheep that could all quite possibly be worth 1500 guineas each. We now know that we need to look after them, pamper them, take care of them.

A thought even crossed my mind that I should put padlocks on the gates in case we get unwanted visitors. By those market prices I reckon we have around £15,000 tied up in our tiny flock.

Sod the messing around with sponges, let's just get on with looking after these sheep properly and having the best Border Leicester flock we can grow. Then let's get back to Carlisle, where we already have a reputation for our Whitebred stock, and see what we can do with them, our own stock in the sale ring.

We ended up with our Border Leicesters scanning at 191 per cent averaging nearly two per ewe in-lamb, with one set of quads, a couple of triplets, one single and two barren, the rest with two.

They finished lambing just before finishing this book, having been scattered over six weeks.

We have had 14 pedigree Border Leicester lambs that have survived, four of them ewe lambs. We can now get started with selection policy over what stays, what goes to sales, maybe what even goes to a show this year.

We will give the barren ewes another chance of becoming in-lamb this year because they are still young and we can't understand why they were not in-lamb, apart from perhaps our own mismanagement of them earlier. We will also have the four ewe lambs that will come into the breeding flock.

More of a dilemma will be what to do with the boys, the tup lambs. Because we are new we won't know which will be good or not so good in order to be sold as breeding tup lambs, but we think that because of the high quality we have started with, that we should be able to produce two or three good tup lambs from the crop.

We will be looking for assistance from the breed society in the characteristics we need to be looking for before we make a decision over which need to be castrated.

It's normal policy to castrate most tup lambs at birth except for those the breeder thinks will be good as tups. At some point of the year we will then definitely have to separate the boys from the girls until we know which boys will meet the breed criteria. At that point, once we have selected, the rest will either be sold as entire tups or castrated.

But all of the ewe lambs will be kept for breeding providing they look the part and don't have any defects. Our aim in the breeding ewe world is to produce our own flock replacements and to sell shearlings. That means we won't see much of an income from those until they are about a year and a half.

We have registered our pedigree sheep prefix with the society, but unlike our cattle that have the Springview prefix our Border Leicester sheep are under the Thornton Hill prefix as Springview was already taken.

That's the prefix to look out for at the shows when we get to them!

We are also now members of the Society of Border Leicester Sheep Breeders. We have been members of societies of the other breeds we've had on the farm and I think that is important. It shows your commitment. When we are a little more established I would like to host a society event here, as we are doing later this year with the Whitebreds, but first let's get ourselves a little more familiar with our breed.

We now have 15 Border Leicester breeding ewes to be put to Quartermaster in August this year and I will probably also buy some Hebridean breeding ewes to start properly on the Mule using the Border Leicester tup.

We are looking forward to the future with our Border Leicesters now that we know their value and now that I've hopefully learned a few very valuable lessons. But I'm sure there will be more lessons still to learn!

CHAPTER 27

DONKEYS & GOATS

Your Goats Are Out!

As a child I used to love seeing and riding the donkeys on the beach at Scarborough. My favourite donkey was called Wendy. Do you remember the days when all the donkeys on the beach had their names on them, like on a big strap or belt?

Wendy was a grey. I just think donkeys are the most endearing creatures and now that I had my own farm, I thought maybe I could do my bit for them as you hear of cruelty to them around the world.

And you can't have one donkey, you have to have two to give them companionship. It was another species of animal too. I was filling my farm with life in those first months. I'd bought them from a lady just north of Thirsk.

Kate was horrified! I won't say the actual word she said here because my wife is a lady, but suffice to say that it was along the lines of why I had acquired them! I think you get the gist.

I just thought they would be nice to have, and they were. I loved that people who walked along our country lane couldn't help themselves but smile when they saw them. My donkeys.

I'd had this romantic, daft idea that kids would come in the summertime and ride them, but the problem with that was you couldn't get anywhere near them.

The lady I'd got them from, who was a customer at

Green's, had been trying to rehome the mother and son and I could soon see why. The mother was okay but the son, that's a jack donkey, really was seriously loopy. He would kick and bite.

What I'd not taken into account (that's another line for saying I'd not thought things through, by the way) was that donkeys also eat grass. And we didn't have a lot of grass to go around with me buying 50 sheep and them having 75 lambs, plus a growing herd, all within the first year. It's a wonder we had any grass after 12 months!

This whole time, thinking back now, was a really strange time of my life and I totally understand Kate's frustration, especially as my bloody donkeys stayed in the same paddock as Kate's horse and were eating all the grass. We ended up having to buy more hay for the horse.

Oh, and then there were the goats!

When I'd gone to pick up the donkeys, this same lady also had goats, pygmy goats. The most adorable things. I came home with two donkeys, four pygmy goats and a billy. There's no wonder Kate went ever so slightly wild at me!

You've no idea how high a little pygmy goat can jump! Unfortunately, our neighbours soon could! We had these stock fences all around them and they just jumped over them. They were always getting out wherever I put them.

'Your goats are out!'

This was the most common text, phone call or shriek we received at the time, dependent on which direction they had taken off.

They were the ultimate escapees! And they loved flowers! They loved our flowers and I'm pretty damned certain that if they'd ever made it further than the country lane and had made it into the village it would have been gardening carnage. I don't think my nearest and dearest neighbours would have been opening up their gardens for one of those Open Gardens events if my leaping goats had come to call.

Luckily enough for Kate and me, they never made it that far, but we had a few near misses. I think the locals were starting to wonder who this madman was, seemingly constantly hurtling after errant pigs, sheep, donkeys and goats across fields and up and down lanes!

We also increased in goat numbers quite rapidly as the four pygmy goats all had kids more or less straight away after arriving. They kidded on their own too. It was amazing to see these hardy little kids.

I do miss them. They were very nice animals that you could sit down with and they would let you stroke them and they were fun to watch and play with. You could put a picnic table in a field and they would spend the next hour jumping on to it and jumping off it. They were really fun.

My only personal drawback was the billy! I don't know whether you've ever smelled a billy goat but I hadn't until we had him. He just stank. It was rank. Absolutely disgusting. Apparently, they cover themselves in urine to attract the females. Guys, I don't recommend this as something you should try! I never have, just in case you're wondering, Caprice!

In the end I put my sensible head on and let them go, but I wish I'd kept them. Goats are such playful animals that I can honestly say having them around was great for my wellbeing. They made me smile, all of their antics, including their escapology!

CHAPTER 28

PIGS

The Sow That Had Just One Piglet

All sows produce multiple numbers of piglets. It is the law. That's what happens. Right?

Not exactly.

I've had sows farrow 14 as one of my current sows Cindy has recently. I've had one sow farrow 15, but that was Lulu, the world's clumsiest sow who managed to obliterate half her litter within a week! And much to my own embarrassment, I've had a sow that only bore one piglet. I'll go through that again because it doesn't get any better or any less amazing every time I write it or say it.

This sow had ONE piglet! Unheard of. I have never been so embarrassed in my life. Me! A pig farmer. Someone who knows about pigs.

Pigs have litters. That's more than one and more than two, three or four. Fair enough some breeds aren't as prolific as others, but ONE bloody piglet!

Kate thought this was the most hilarious thing. This was a massive sow, I kid you not. She was big. I kept telling myself the same thing after it was clear there were no more to come, that I've had cows and sheep that have had more than that.

Normally, I'm keen to show people around the farm to show off the breeding of my cows, ewes and sows, but not this time! What was I supposed to say? 'This is my sow – and this is her ONE piglet!' It was never going to happen.

Maybe the poor old sow had some kind of infection after having been served? All I thought at the time, given that this was fairly early on in being here at Spring View, was that if this is what it was going to be like having Oxford Sandy & Blacks that we maybe ought to look at a different breed.

We did actually dabble a bit with pig breeds at first. I was trying Saddlebacks at around the same time. I'd bought a couple from Lyn Arrowsmith at Raskelf, because I'd thought that it might be nice to have a couple of rare breeds or even more.

All different colours running around the place, but the problem is for every pedigree breed you have, if you're going to breed, you need a pedigree boar and that causes all sorts of logistical problems in keeping boars apart and the breeds apart, but we settled on the plum pudding pigs.

I'd bought the Saddleback pigs from Lyn in-pig to a Saddleback boar, so I never had a Saddleback boar on our farm and once they'd had their litters I sold the sows to someone who wanted to keep Saddlebacks and concentrated on my wonderful Oxford Sandy & Blacks.

We've only ever had one other breed on the farm and that was some Welsh in-pig sows. I'd bought them in 2021 when I'd been planning for my farm open day that I'd had to cancel in 2020. In the end it fell the same way, a victim of the pandemic regulations. I wanted to have a couple of litters available for my show day. I've sold them since.

The Oxford Sandy & Black is here to stay at Spring View. It is the most beautiful, docile, endearing animal that is very friendly and so lovely to deal with. It is the real smallholder's pig! And it fits for two really important criteria for those of us with small farms, in that the pigs are gorgeous creatures to look at and they produce lovely meat.

And while this ONE piglet was a major disappointment

that it didn't have any brothers or sisters it grew into this most enormous pig! And why wouldn't it? It had everything! It must have been in little piggie heaven when it was born. Teats to suck left right and centre!

I can just see my dad laughing, up there! I don't think in all his days, or my granddad's, they ever had a sow that gave birth to just one piglet, but then would they have told me if they had? Probably not if they were anything like me!

In case you're wondering, yes, the sow didn't last much after that. She made for very tasty pork, ham and sausages!

You don't think I was going to give her an opportunity to embarrass me again, do you?

CHAPTER 29

PIGS

Oxford Sandy & Blacks

While we have made a point of having breeds that we like the look of on the farm, attractive sheep, cattle and pigs, they're not just here to look pretty. They all have to pay their way. Our cattle and sheep breeds are now set up to primarily supply other breeders, but some of the stock will still go for meat and that's certainly what happens with the Oxford Sandy & Blacks too.

Reading this book, in places you might think I'm a little too sentimental and soft about my animals at times, but part of what I'm intending to do here is to show that while these rare breeds are lovely animals they will not survive without being consumed as meat.

I think it is important that people understand where their food comes from and the breeds that are around today, from those that are hugely popular in the food chain to those that are not and explain how this can be rectified.

Breeds of cattle, sheep and pigs have become rare because people have largely stopped eating the meat from them. That can be down to a number of factors including fat content, the influence of continental breeds that are known for producing leaner meat, and also the fashion, but the fact is, that I'm trying to get across, is that to keep these breeds alive and to increase their numbers there has to be an increase in consumption of their meat. If you don't eat the meat of rare breed animals the rare breeds will eventually become extinct.

The Oxford Sandy & Black produces the most beautiful dark coloured meat with more fat through it than pork or bacon you might buy from elsewhere. It's very flavoursome.

Sows are the mainstay of any pig breeding enterprise. They are either put to the boar or they receive AI (artificial insemination).

If you get two litters a year you're doing well from a rare breed, whereas pigs that have been specifically bred for a much more commercial system with huge numbers of sows on site would normally average around 2.4 litters per year and an average litter size of 10–14.

While we have had a few decent size litters, I don't like to push ours. We are not a huge commercial operation. We like to give our sows a more relaxed life in natural surroundings and I keep mine outside in one area of a field separated by three paddocks for the pigs, from May until October. It's a proper living for a pig, in a field, with a wallow, its own water and a pig arc.

On the side of the pig arc I put up some posts with plywood on top, which acts as a veranda, giving them shade during the sun.

If I put the boar in with the sows every now and again it tends to sort them out, otherwise the sows tend to not get on too well when they are together, but there's plenty of room in the paddock for them to get away from each other. I try to leave one of the paddocks to rest so that some greenery can come back from all of the rooting that pigs do naturally.

I have a building where I bring them inside for winter on straw.

Our current sow team includes Cindy, Polly, Lucy and Molly with a new arrival due from Wales in April, Gertie.

She's in-pig and from the Gertrude line. There's also Jack, our year-old boar.

Lucy had 10 and has reared 10; Cindy has just given her first litter that saw her with 14 at the start and reared 12; Polly has just had her second litter and reared 10; and Molly had 10 and reared 9. All except Polly are gilts, which means it is their first time and that means it is quite a young sow herd at the moment. The four sows are all from different herds.

It's a young and new team all round on the breeding side at present as we also have Jack our new young boar who we bought from breeder Mary Benfield in Wales. Jack has been responsible for our current litters. He's clearly doing his job well as our litter numbers are very healthy at the moment.

Cindy ended up with 12 really lovely, healthy pigs after having laid on 2. Hers is the best litter we've had so far and shows their potential and that we are batting at the right end of the breeding table, unlike when we started with the sow that had just ONE piglet.

I was a sow inseminator many years ago when I worked for Nitrovit at their semen collection centre at Skipton-on-Swale. We collected it from the boars, put it into bottles and I went on to the farms to inseminate the sows while it was fresh.

Our Oxford Sandy & Black semen comes from the Deerpark Stud, the Rare Breed AI station in Northern Ireland, and if you order before noon it arrives on the farm in the first-class post the next morning.

There is often a degree of hilarity when it comes, bringing about good-natured conversation as the postman delivers it in this white box that is marked up 'Boar Semen' and has these 2ft-long catheters strapped to the top of it.

It's quite an odd-looking package and we do get some strange looks when it is handed over, especially if the postman is someone new to the round!

It's a good service and always arrives fresh. It will have been collected by the centre on the morning of the ordering, on the farm the next day and has a preservative that keeps it fresh for three or four days.

Rare Breed AI centres will by their nature be very limited in the bloodlines that you can receive as there may be only one or at best perhaps two Oxford Sandy & Black boars standing at any one time, so that's the one you have to take.

Jack was certainly enjoying himself earlier this year. I don't always get to see the action, because I'm at Green's, and so it is better to have the boar with the sows because then I know they will be covered. I did see Jack having some piggy fun with Lucy after we weaned her though.

Jack's also been working nearby at Monk Park Farm visitor attraction at Bagby, where he has serviced two Oxford Sandy & Black females that were born from our previous boar Barney. I'd loaned Jack to them because it is important that all rare breed enterprises try their best to help each other.

Barney had worked on our sows for a couple of years after having come to us from Southend. He's now working on another group of sows near Thirsk.

Every gilt needs to satisfy the breed specifications before it can be registered as an Oxford Sandy & Black, which is very important as it adds to the gilt's value. The breed specifications include having 14 teats all evenly placed in line and correct markings with ideally four white socks, a white stripe on the nose and nice, even markings throughout. It mustn't have any swirly bits on its coat.

Our main market for our pigs at present is selling as many weaners as we can at 10–12 weeks old for people who want to either rear them for meat or who want to breed from them, keeping one or two gilts as replacements from time to time.

We seem to have developed a demand as we constantly receive messages from people wanting weaners, either from breeders, butchers or farm shops. The Oxford Sandy & Black has a growing reputation and we're finding our name is getting better known too.

We try to farrow so that we can get the weaners away in summertime because our customers want to buy them through the summer. They don't want to have to deal with them through winter.

We usually get around £50 for a 12-week-old weaner, which is quite good and what I consider a fair amount for both myself and the buyer, either the next breeder or the person who will take them on to pork, bacon and all other meats associated with the pig of which there are many.

They are all birth notified through the British Pig Association (BPA) of which we are members. We notify them of new litters, the numbers born to this particular sow and then I am allocated numbers for each piglet. Then we put a tag in each ear so that those pigs all have their own number for traceability purposes.

When they go as weaners to the next breeder or person who will take them on to pork or sausages, or whatever, they can then sell them or eat them as Oxford Sandy & Black pedigree, birth notified meat. The real thing.

That means it will attract a premium because people know where it has come from and that it is pedigree. I think the majority of our customers are keeping them through summer and into autumn before sending them to pork for their own use.

Through the breed society we have recently been getting people asking whether we have breeding stock and as this book was being written we had six boar pigs that were approaching pork weight from a litter that farrowed in 2021.

A couple of them are looking perhaps good enough to be sold as breeding boars, which we haven't done at all as yet, but as we've now become better known we may now be in a position where we have boars available which should realise around £200 to £300. Whether it happens this time or next time is no matter. It will just be good when it does.

It would be some achievement to think that we have produced a boar, sow or gilt that can go on to another breeding herd.

I am really proud of what we have achieved so far, but that doesn't mean I intend to sit back. I still want us to get better and I want us to create this really good gene pool of Oxford Sandy & Blacks.

CHAPTER 30

POTATOES

Potato Pie

When I'm in our fields here at Spring View I sometimes think back to those days with my granddad when I'd be out with him at Oaklea Farm.

At hay-time I'd be out cutting the hay and gathering it up with a fork to put it into mounds that would be collected later on.

There was certainly spring barley as there was no winter corn in those days. I remember the barley very clearly because of the cutting with a horse-drawn binder that cut the corn into sheaths. They then came off the back of the binder and you stacked them in stooks – stalks of corn with their heads still on. The binder didn't thrash the grain, it just cut it and then gathered it all up with a horse and trailer, brought it back to the farm and stacked it into a Dutch barn.

When all the harvest was gathered in by mid-September there would be a point between then and Christmas when the thrashing machine would come round and a team of men would come, the sheaths of corn would be taken from the Dutch barn and put in to be thrashed.

Thrashing Day was a big day in the calendar. There would be 20 men on the farm and the big thing I remember was Nanna Bertha making all these wonderful pastries for what the men called 'Lowance' at 11 o'clock, like we now know as elevenses, and dinner at midday or 1 o'clock.

Nanna fed everybody well and I shall never forget being amazed at the table full of food.

Thrashing teams would go from farm to farm and I don't think they charged their time because it was made up of farmers in the area and you all did your turn on the team. The guy who owned the thrashing machine would be paid.

They'd be put in by a man on top of the machine who would cut the string that bound the sheaths. Others would be sorting out the bags of grain when they were filled.

These were 16-stone bags and then had to be carried up the granary steps. The grain would later be sold to a grain merchant with some kept on farm for milling. Granddad milled his own feed for his horses and cattle.

The other crop I remember Granddad growing was potatoes. He wouldn't grow a lot, maybe three or four acres, but in those days the half-term school holiday became potato picking time for all the kids.

In those days potatoes wouldn't be picked out of the ground with a machine as they are today. They were brought out by a spinner. The horse would pull this thing that had two metal wheels going around, turning the ground up and the potatoes then fell out on top with a team of us kids walking behind with wire baskets picking them up.

The potatoes would be put onto the cart and would be taken to a field where a potato pie was made to store the potatoes.

First you would lay a bed of straw. This would provide the insulation for the crop, avoiding moisture getting to the potatoes. Then you would tip the potatoes on top building them up like a triangular pyramid shape or, with the length it was, like a Toblerone shape. It would end up something like 50 yards long, about 8ft high in the middle and 12ft wide. It was quite a sight, but it was how potatoes were stored at the time outside. After the potatoes had been deposited you then put a wheat straw thatch again over the potatoes and then shovel soil over the straw and all by hand.

It was done this way because in those days it was before refrigeration or controlled storage came in. You wouldn't sell all of your crop straight away, so you needed to store them to be sold later.

The Potato Pie was known right across the country.

I don't think I will ever make one myself but having my own farm and walking around it sometimes brings back all of those memories. They were fantastic times of my childhood, which is where all of this we have today started.

It was Granddad Bob and his horses Tommy and Laddie, my dad, Nanna Bertha's home cooking, wuzzletops, mangelwurzles and Granddad's pigs. All now memories from long ago, but they all come back to me here.

But Potato Pie, maybe I should grow some just to have a go at it one day!

CHAPTER 31

CATTLE

Highlanders

I'm known as Farmer Chris by lots of people who've seen me on the telly, including some other farmers. I've been up at Borderway Mart a few times and had people say 'You're Farmer Chris' and it is nice to be recognised, but Kate has a different name for me, especially when she quite understandably despairs.

That's when I get my Sunday name, Christopher.

This is how Kate describes those early days of when we came to the farm when I was buying what must have seemed like anything that moved on four legs:

'Christopher decides to rear calves. Christopher buys calves. Looking at our book we had an awful lot. Christopher decides he wants to buy 50 sheep. Christopher buys 50 sheep. I do despair at times. He just gets carried away.'

And of course, she's right.

I did decide to rear calves and I also decided to buy other cattle in addition to our Whitebred Shorthorns. At one time I used to go on my iPhone on an evening and visit the Preloved site and if I could find a cow that I thought looked alright I'd go and buy it. That's how I bought some Highlanders and a Hereford-cross cow.

Oh, eh up, here's Kate again:

'You're talking through your bottom again. You just went to that man near York where you bought Moilie from to buy the Hereford-cross.'

Ah, that's right. I'd bought Moilie and then I'd bought a Hereford-cross heifer from this chap who has a lot of cattle at the aerodrome at Elvington.

The Irish Moiled is the only surviving domestic breed of cattle in Northern Ireland and is a dual-purpose breed for dairy and beef, but has developed a great reputation for its beef, particularly in the UK, and I wanted to have some of my own beef, to try it.

Moilie was a lovely steer. Oh, hold on, Kate's back.

'He was when we got him calmed down.'

Yes, right again. It took a short while, but then he'd let me rub his head and he was good. He went on to become a fantastic beef animal and truly his beef was the best I've ever tasted in my life.

We bulled the Hereford-cross heifer with one of our Whitebred Shorthorn bulls. Here's Kate again.

'She had a really pretty calf and we sold her. We actually made a bit of money there.'

And that was that with those two, but let me tell you about our Highlanders.

I'd thought we ought to have a couple of Highland cattle. We've got a smallholding, won't they look nice with their shaggy coats and horns and everything. I knew they would look good in the field as people walked by.

I found a couple about ten miles away and bought them. One was a chestnut/dun colour, the other was black and they were in-calf to a Salers.

What I'd not been aware of was their condition and looking back I really shouldn't have bought them, but they were relatively cheap and I'd liked the idea of having them around.

Our problems started as the black one Nellie was just so weak that she just about fell off the trailer on getting here. Connie the chestnut was a little better. I thought that if I looked after them, got some flesh on them, they'd be okay, and we would at least have two calves that we could sell afterwards.

Typically for me things didn't go to plan, and also very sadly, Nellie slipped her calf, but we did at least manage to get her back in-calf.

Both cows looked much stronger, fitter and better all round after they'd been at Spring View a year. And they were a wonderful sight. I had them with my Whitebreds and had this idea about putting a Whitebred on to them.

Had I thought this through? She's back.

'No, you hadn't.'

The Highlanders were getting horny! And I don't mean in that way! I'd just thought the cross of a Highland cow and a Whitebred Shorthorn bull was a great marriage. But the problem really was their horns.

They were butting all the Whitebreds with them and then they were constantly getting their horns stuck in the ring feeders.

Another lesson. Cattle with horns need a different ring feeder.

We sold Nellie and her calf to this really nice couple who had seen her on the Preloved site and we kept Connie a bit longer and had her horns cut off, one of the jobs I asked Julian (Norton) to come and do. We eventually sold her to a farm in Chop Gate between Helmsley and Stokesley.

So, you see, it has not all been about Whitebred Shorthorns at Spring View!

CHAPTER 32

CATTLE

Whitebred Shorthorns – A Very Rare Sale

Building up a pedigree herd from scratch can take some time unless you have the money to buy say ten or a dozen cows and heifers straight away. You can do what I was doing and buy two pedigree cows; and then fiddle around with some bucket rearing of any variety of calf, which I was doing more to satisfy my need for lots of activity, lots of noise on the farm, but that wasn't going to get us anywhere fast.

I hadn't minded.

Having Lochie and Bertha was great. I'd been a little disappointed when they'd both had bull calves though, because I'd wanted to grow my herd from what we produced and that wasn't going to happen if all my cows produced were boys! We needed girls!

We'd had a better strike rate the following year in 2017 when Bertha had produced Tabitha, and Elizabeth, who we'd bought in-calf from Helen Chard, produced Lady Kathryn, but they wouldn't be ready to start producing calves until 2020. It's a long process, and you don't know what is going to happen to them in the meantime.

We'd added to our herd with another cow purchase, Northwood Catherine, in November 2017 and that gave us a team of Lochie, Bertha, Elizabeth and Catherine all in-calf for 2018.

Calving is always an exciting time for Kate and me. We just want things to go well, like any expectant parents, but because I desperately wanted to grow the herd I wanted to see more girls.

Elizabeth had Victoria; Bertha had Alice; we had a bull calf out of Catherine, called Tristan, so named after my favourite character from the original TV series *All Creatures Great & Small*; but we were to suffer our first loss of a calf with Lochie.

This had never happened to us before. It was a light, sunny June morning and I'd gone up the field to check on her. I could see her walking up and down alongside this hedge. It was as if she didn't know what to do with herself. Then I saw this white thing lying next to her.

My heart started to pound and I began running up the hill fearing the worst. As I approached, I knew. You know, they show all these lovely videos of animals being born on television these days and they are wonderful. It's a great thing. But there is nothing more tragic than seeing something that has just come out of a womb but has no life.

I blame myself. I should have had her inside or I should have been up earlier. It was about 4 in the morning, but even if I'd been there a little earlier it could have been alive.

The really sad story is that you can't just leave the dead calf there. It has to go. You can imagine the kind of publicity a farmer can get if any deadstock is just left lying around. And so, it's an ignominious ending as you chuck the poor thing into a wheelbarrow and tootle off down the field with the cow following you.

You need to look after your cow because she is now lactating with the expectation of feeding her new calf, but now it's not there. She's also got her own emotional upheaval of her missing calf. She's been through just over 9 months of carrying her baby which she has expected to look after.

You can't leave her with a full bag of milk and no calf. Again, our learning curve hit a new upward trajectory as we learned later that the best thing we could have done for her at that moment was to go and get her a calf that would suck on her teats.

We had tried to look after her and I had given her some treatment but we hadn't known really what to do for the best, and consequently she got mastitis.

Crikey! We were going from bad to worse again, but that just reinforces what we already now knew, that there is so much to keep learning. It's all very well getting excited about calving, but when it goes drastically wrong you've got to know what to do. We learned from this.

We actually thought we had done the right thing at first by treating her, but we hadn't managed it at all properly. We'd let her go out again into the field because we thought she was wanting to be out with the rest of the herd, but by doing that she then started producing more milk, which then led to the mastitis.

After that had happened we then couldn't get Lochie in-calf again and that was her time over for us. Instead of adding to our herd we were subtracting!

But then good fortune came my way!

My good friend Richard Greenwood, of whom I owe a huge debt of gratitude for his constant help on the farm – the man with the Kramer – told me he knew there was a Whitebred cow for sale at York livestock market.

I didn't believe it could be right but was excited that it was. Whitebreds don't just come up for sale like that, in a normal weekday sale. What it meant was, if it really was happening, that there might be an opportunity to pick something up without other Whitebred breeders around.

I rang the Whitebred Society to ask whether they knew there was a Whitebred cow for sale. I thought they might have been aware of some kind of sale, but maybe with it just being one they weren't.

They weren't.

Off I went the following day to Murton, home of York

livestock market, and when I got there it wasn't just one Whitebred Shorthorn for sale! And what an amazing day I had!

Ben Ledi Duke was there, only one of the top Whitebred bulls in the country. I didn't know just how important he was until I rang the man who'd bred him, Donald Hendry, one of the top breeders and a fount of all knowledge about the Whitebreds. I rang him from York. By now I was beyond myself with nervous energy about my 'find'. Wow! This could really set us on our way.

Donald said that if I could buy him to do so because he was so well bred and held lots of genetics that would be useful to me. This was a bull. I'd been thinking cows and building up my herd until this point, but this could really take us places. Ben Ledi Duke in my herd! Oh yes!

Because these Whitebred Shorthorns were at York in a regular weekday stores sale there weren't the buyers that would have been around the ring if they had been at a pedigree sale. They'd been up for sale there because the chap who'd had them had needed to sell them quickly.

Everything had fallen my way!

I came home with Ben Ledi Duke; two cows both in-calf; and a calf. That's six lives coming back to Spring View. And I got the lot for £1500! I had a field day. Nobody else was there with any desire for the breed to bid against me and all they were making was culling money. I'd bought some cheap stock before but never like this, this was pedigree stock that was going to help me.

The two cows were Callyheath Queen, who we called Queenie; and Callyheath Margery with her six-month-old calf Callyheath Heather. Only Queenie of the three was already registered.

But, sadly, it wasn't all good news.

The really good news though was that we had got an absolute steal with the purchase of Ben Ledi Duke.

CHAPTER 33

CATTLE

Whitebred Shorthorns – The Donald Hendry Story

We are now ardent members of the Premium Cattle Health Scheme run by SRUC from St Boswell's. It is one of the largest and most respected cattle health certification standards and the reason we are members is that my main priority is not just to breed top quality pedigree livestock, but for everything in the farm to have high health status.

At first I was buying something I saw that was cheap, thinking I'll have that. Bloody Irish Moileds, Hereford-crosses. I hadn't given a first thought to what stock I'd be bringing in and from where, as my neighbour had pointed out too.

What brought it all home to me and really told me I had to stop all this was when we had our first health tests after having bought Callyheath Queen. It wasn't good.

Queenie was carrying Johne's Disease, it's a chronic, contagious wasting disease in cattle. She had to go immediately. She went to Thirsk livestock market as she couldn't be sold as a breeder.

Yes, I'd been lucky getting Ben Ledi Duke, but I still hadn't given a thought to checking on the health status of the animals I was buying at York that day and because of that I'd brought back something infectious to the farm.

This now makes everything come very clear in my mind. Christopher. It's now me using my Sunday name.

Christopher has to stop wheeling and dealing in everything whatsoever just because he likes them and thinks he'll make a shilling or two.

I made the decision to stay with Whitebreds, ensure I only bought from those whose herds were registered, had all the necessary documentation and were totally clean. It was now the time to do it all properly, all the way.

But things were already about to turn even worse.

Two of our cows tested positive for Infectious Bovine Rhinitis (IBR). The word 'disease' is enough. We knew that to become IBR clear we had to let both Bertha and Catherine go.

I was really struggling with this because Bertha was my favourite cow and we made the decision we would keep them both for a second check. They both came back positive a second time and have both gone now, although Bertha's was a much sadder end.

These results had come after Bertha, Elizabeth, Queenie and Margery had all calved in 2019.

Fortune again turned our way when, in 2019, Donald Hendry told me he was selling his farm and moving to a smaller place and he had quite a few cattle to sell.

Now this really was special. These really were top-class pedigree stock and these would definitely set our herd up for the future. I ended up saying to Kate that I wanted to buy them because they really were so special and they would never come on the market again. I couldn't resist. There were 8 beautiful, top-class cows.

Heck! Kate's back!

'Tell Chris how you paid for them, Christopher. Because you know what my reaction was. How are you paying for them?'

Okay, I went to my mother.

'But to be completely accurate we had sold three in-calf heifers in the spring sale at Carlisle.'

So, we had some money coming in, but it certainly wasn't enough to buy this quality.

Donald's cows came to us in March 2020. They were all in-calf and the first to calf was Katrine Cassi at around 4 o'clock in the morning. And I was struggling!

I had my arm in her and it just didn't feel right. The vet came. Cassi managed to calve but it was badly deformed and dead. Our first calf from Donald's brilliant cows.

Not what we'd had in mind at all, but at least we had learned from what had happened to Lochie and went to our local dairy farm to get a calf to put on Cassi.

Sally Banks runs the dairy farm's calf unit, where Sally and her husband John and John's brother Roger also run their farm on high health status too. I bought the biggest calf she had. He was a British Blue out of a Holstein dairy cow and we called him Woolly Bear. I put him in the back of my pickup and straight back to Cassi. All of a sudden we've this lovely bull calf sucking on all 4 cylinders. We had at least learned our lesson from the Lochie experience.

When I told Donald what had happened I found out even more about the type of gentleman he is. He gave us a heifer, Cassi's heifer she'd calved the previous year. What a wonderful thing. Such a gesture. We picked her up later in the year.

We bought another heifer calf from Donald when we visited and then later he told me of two in-calf heifers he was also disposing of – the Penelopes.

In total we bought 12 breeding animals from Donald and that has really expanded the herd because with the in-calf heifers that brought us 20 Whitebred Shorthorn lives.

We calved 15 cows and heifers in 2020 and what an amazing thing! There were 10 heifer calves born. This was a real joy and certainly brought a big smile to my face.

I'm even worse than any expectant father when my cows are calving. The first thing I ever want to do is open their legs and see what's there. Ah, it's a heifer! Now that is still the most fantastic feeling.

From a standing start of two Whitebred Shorthorns we now have 50. And my biggest thanks for getting us there must go to the gentleman that is Donald Hendry.

CHAPTER 34

CATTLE

Whitebred Shorthorns – Kitty & Henry

Our 2021 foray up to Carlisle was both a triumph and a disaster – and also presented a little logistical nightmare along the way.

One of the things we've discovered through our pedigree journey with Whitebred bulls is that, just like the society has always known, the bulls are great for using as a crossing sire on to other breeds. The reason why the Bluegrey has remained is largely down to the Whitebred. It's a market that we've yet to fully tap ourselves, but with the size of herd we have now it is one that we are looking at closely and starting to target.

In Autumn 2021 we'd taken six animals – 3 heifers and 3 bulls. We'd got our local livestock hauliers Bell's to take them up to Carlisle. Kate and I were stopping over in a hotel. We finally got there, exhausted, after seeing them unloaded and having washed them ready for the morning.

It's usually a fast and furious start to the morning of a show and then sale with every kind of preening and prepping equipment being used to pamper and buff and blow dry and fluff up the cattle so that they look magnificent – and they do!

Kate always makes a great job of the animals so that they are all perfection. There's foam, waxing, combing, getting their coats looking the most spectacular possible. The end of the tail is always buffed up. And remember these are white animals, so you have to be particularly keen as any mark will show up.

Ian Park, ex-herdsman for Gerald Turton's Upsall herd of Beef Shorthorns, was going to show them for us. We'd done all we could the night before and next morning. In the lead up to a show you also halter train to make sure your animals are walking correctly and looking great. It's such a big job. Hats off to all of those who show their animals so many times at shows up and down the country for months on end. It takes time to get it right.

And get it right we did!

Springview Kitty won her class. And then she went on to be Reserve Champion. A female had never done as well as that before in the breed's show. We received the platter. It was such a fantastic feeling that something we had bred had done it. And we'd done it in such a relatively short space of time. What an achievement.

The bulls didn't sell as well as I had hoped. Two of them, Donald and Christopher (I wonder where we got that name from?), sold for 1000 guineas each, but Henry didn't reach that figure, so I decided to take him home. In my opinion he'd been the best of the three and I thought I'd either use him in my herd or would take him back in this year's sales (2022).

We'd had an up-and-down day, but the high of achieving Reserve Champion meant we had smiles on our faces. We were winners. I love winning, achieving. I want to be the best at whatever I do. Nothing is ever really good enough. I'm always looking for something, something different to try and improve.

And this time the first thing I needed to improve on was my logistics management.

Now, the problem with having taken six animals wasn't a problem at all, but what I'd not thought through this time was that I'd decided not to sell one of them.

What this meant was that taking any animal back home from a livestock market means, because we are a high health herd, that it has to come back into quarantine for at least two weeks before it can go back in the herd.

But that wasn't the main problem. This meant I had one animal that needed to get home – and no means of transportation.

Oh my! Here we go again!

I hadn't thought for one minute that I'd be taking anything home. I had no trailer and a ruddy great bull to get back. I asked around at the mart but nobody was going to Thirsk or even near that had any form of transport available.

There was only one thing for it. I had to get back to Thornton on the Hill and then set off back to Carlisle to bring Springview Henry back to Thornton on the Hill again. Just a combined three-trip run for me of 330 miles at two hours in a car and two and a half hours per run with a trailer. Seven hours of my life down and up and down again.

Kate and I set off for Spring View at about midday. We got home, the first time around 2pm. We just had time to watch George William, the bull we'd bred that was for sale, go into the ring on live stream while I had a quick brew. I then set off immediately with the trailer.

I'd had a good run and was back at Carlisle for 4.30 and I was back on the road with Henry loaded. Funnily enough I was happy that I'd not let him go.

I was on my way back to Spring View. It was Friday teatime on the M6 coming south near Penrith. I'd normally come across the A66 but saw the queue and came off at Tebay instead a bit further south. I took the scenic route coming back through Kirkby Stephen. I felt good.

In fact I felt really good, even better, because when I'd returned to Carlisle and was loading Springview Henry, the Whitebred Shorthorn breed secretary Anna Pattinson was on the loading dock.

I'd started apologising to her that I'd not been able to make the latest breed council meeting and she'd said that I hadn't to worry, but there were three things that had been decided at the meeting that she needed to tell me.

First, they wanted me to be in an article in a farming magazine talking about Whitebreds. Second, I'd been nominated as a Whitebred judge. Third, they wanted Kate and me to represent the Whitebred Society at Beef Expo to be held at Darlington livestock market in May 2022 with one of our animals.

Wow! Wow! Wow! No wonder I enjoyed my journey home. What a day!

CHAPTER 35

CATTLE

Belted Galloways – The Runaway Heifer

Kate and I have always admired the Belted Galloway breed, but we had heard they had a reputation for being a bit hard to handle, which is one of the reasons we had decided against them in favour of our Whitebred Shorthorn herd.

However, I had this idea to cross our Ben Ledi Duke onto a 'Beltie' female to produce a great animal with a good carcase which we could sell as prime beef in our store at Thirsk. Had I thought this through? Wait and see!

I made some enquiries through the Belted Galloway Society and found a breeder in Dumfries, Robert McDuff, who had 4 heifers he was looking to sell. One was a red and white (roan) and the others the traditional black and white.

I decided to buy them as long as Robert could deliver them as we didn't have a suitable trailer and I didn't fancy the trip to Dumfries and back with 4 Belties on board. Note not one or two, but four!

It's May 2020 and the Belties are due to be delivered around lunchtime. I had an indoor pen ready for them as I knew they would have to settle down before turning out to grass.

Once the trailer with said Belties arrived my fears were immediately raised as I could not only see the steam coming out of the trailer vents, but I could also hear this cacophonous racket of wild snorting and loud bangs as they violently kicked the side of the trailer. I know what you're thinking. 'Oh, Christopher!'

Robert reversed his trailer into my barn as we prepared for unloading.

"Och! They're a bit lively!" he enthused with a strange wry smile. He was not dissimilar to a Beltie himself, I thought. He had a wild crop of dark hair with streaks of red and grey in it. His beard was long and scruffy and he spoke with a sharp Scottish accent.

I had already paid him by BACS transfer and he seemed keen to get going.

"Keep 'em locked up in here a wee while before you let 'em out," he advised.

Then he was off. I stood there looking at my new purchases and wondered what I had let myself in for.

They truly were 4 beautiful, well-bred and well-marked Belted Galloways and in pristine condition. But something worried me. They were now in the secure pen within my barn, but were they happy? No, not happy at all.

Their ears were pricked and twitched. They were continually snorting and very restless. But, in fairness, they had just travelled from Dumfries to my little farm here in North Yorkshire and would need time to settle. I left them alone and went off hoping they would be calmer before Kate saw them!

The next day they had calmed a little, but when I showed them to Kate I could tell she too was a little concerned.

"Don't turn them out yet!" she instructed, rather more dramatically than I had been anticipating. I was starting to say to myself, 'Oh, Christopher, what have you done?'

They had wild eyes that followed your every move. There was no way I was going into the pen with them! Oh my!

George William, a bull we bred, looking magnificent at Borderway Mart, Carlisle – so proud!

Kate with Roxy at Carlisle

Roxy – our first champion, at Cleveland County Show

Ben Ledi Duke – what an amazing purchase he has been from York

Romeo – I defy anyone not to fall in love with him, here at 3 months old

Beatrice – such a pretty calf

Roxy – a red rosette at Carlisle

Kate knows how to prepare for a show

Bertha – the one-eyed cow!

Bertha – ready for Julian

Texel X lambs on the hill

Doris, Kate's favourite Kerry Hill ewe

Only I could produce
two white lambs out of a
black Hebridean ewe!

I love Hebrideans, me!

Donkeys – I wanted to fill my farm with everything!

Goats – I really did want everything!

Kids – I'm not kidding, but they are!

Belted Galloways – enough said there!

Oxford Sandy & Blacks plus one! How did that Saddleback get there?

Cute or what? Oxford Sandy & Blacks sucking on their mum's teats

Travelling in style! Back out to the field for mum and her litter

Grandson William (son David's son) fills up the wallow

Spa time! And now, time for a wallow!

Just beautiful, Oxford Sandy & Black piglets

Grandchildren Marley and Maisie (son Robert's children)

Julian and Mum

The Yorkshire Vet filming
day with Julian

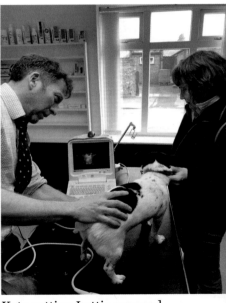

Kate getting Lottie scanned
for pups with Julian

Julian and me at 2 in the morning after bull calf Tristan was born

Tristan being helped out of Springview Kathryn by Julian

Bertha's eye operation by Julian

Peggy and Lottie – very
patriotic dogs!

Christmas dogs – we love our
Jack Russells!

Marley and Maisie (Robert's
children) with Lottie's puppies

Watch out,
here comes trouble!

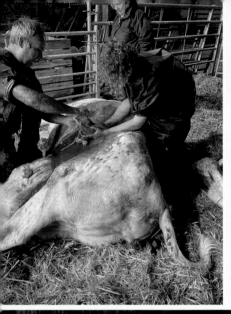

Our wonderful Bishopton Vets performing an immaculate caesarean

Watch out for that milk vein! Shearing taking place without drama!

Bertha had calcium deficiency. I hold my hands up when necessary!

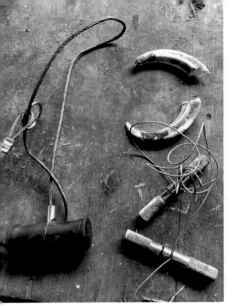

Pig tusk removal kit –
just ask Barney!

Making piggies kit –
just ask our postman!

Got to scratch that itch, you
know!

Snow plough time?

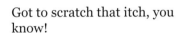

Book signing at Green's – my first book!

Advertising Green's is snow joke!

Our Dave! This man is Green's!

Racehorse owner! Me with Colin. He won quite a few

Caprice. What a lady! She still keeps in touch

Megan who went on to win the *The X Factor: Celebrity 2019*

Mum! Crikey, I've driven her to drink too!

'Oh Christopher!' Kate turns to drink!

Kate and Me in Jamaica – before I was propelled into the air!

Grandson Maddox (Robert's son)

Kate with Lorna

My greatest TV moment: Peter Davison and me, filming
A Christmas Carol for *The Yorkshire Vet*

My greatest TV comedy mate & show partner:
Stephen Bailey came to visit Spring View Farm

We brought a couple of our cows into a pen next to them in the hope they would settle a bit quicker. This seemed to work and a week later we decided to let them into a field at the back of the barn with some other cows.

They seemed happy with this and proceeded to run off at great pace, bucking and kicking and snorting with their tails stuck up in the air.

Then, crunch time. Would they stop at the fence? Phew! Yes, they did.

We left them in the field to settle, with some of our far more demure Whitebred Shorthorn cows. After a week we decided to move them to be with their intended male partner, Duke. The reason for their purchase.

Rounding them up to load them into our trailer and transport them the 2 miles to the field we had rented for the summer was not the easiest task.

I'd had a plan. I'd left the gates open into the barn and had put some food down in the hope they may come in on their own.

Of course, this didn't work. In the end it took Richard (Greenwood) and Kate, two builders who were doing some work at our house and the use of some gates, to get them shifted into the barn, then onto the trailer.

The journey took five minutes. We had a few Whitebred cows and Duke already there, so we knew the Belties would have company. It was really important to give these two-year-old animals the company of older, more sensible cows to calm them.

It was a lovely sunny morning as we drove into the field and shut the gate behind us. What could possibly go wrong?

But I could tell the heifers were not happy again. It was bedlam within the trailer.

"Let them out quick," Kate instructed nervously.

As I pulled the back gate of the trailer down the two

inside folding gates, which form side barriers when loading, were flung open with an almighty smash!

I fell over to one side and three 'Belties' shot out and ran off to the cows in the field. They weren't the problem.

The fourth must have momentarily turned round in the trailer and had missed the rush of the others. Was she any calmer? Not one bit of it.

She took an enormous leap out of the trailer and headed off in completely the other direction, tail up, snorting, bucking and running like hell before reaching the perimeter hedge and leaping, better than any racehorse, straight over it!

She disappeared into a 50-acre field of winter wheat. Not mine! I don't have any wheat. Oh my!

I looked in horror at what was happening. We had done everything right, hadn't we? That didn't matter now. The stark reality was that we now had an animal running wild and we had to catch it before it reached the road and ran into an oncoming car or it reached the beautiful, manicured gardens of Newburgh Priory only half a mile away.

We hurried back into our vehicle, drove out of the field and unhitched the trailer.

Now, to set the scene for you, the field we rent for the cattle is around 15 acres and is surrounded by hundreds of acres of arable land. There are crops of wheat, oats, barley and oilseed rape and it is part of the Newburgh Priory estate. One beast running wild could cause significant losses.

Thankfully, for the general public's safety, our field is some half a mile or so inland off the main road, but safety would only remain that way if this heifer didn't reach the road.

There is much woodland and game cover crops here too as the estate is a shooting estate. Thousands of game birds are reared here and the gamekeepers have many tracks around the fields where they take the shooting fraternity around during the shooting season. Not good news to be met by a raging heifer!

We decided to ring our good friend Alan Turnbull. He and his father Peter farm on the estate not far away. I told Alan the news. He said he would meet us on one of the keepers tracks to see if we could see it. He reckoned she may head for some cattle in a field near him.

When we met him Alan was standing there looking over a field of oats and pointing.

He said, "She's there, look. Will she come to a feed bucket?"

"Not a chance," I replied.

Alan seemed to think this was hilarious and told us we would just have to leave her to make her own way back to the field.

"We once had one out round here for a week," he announced.

This did me no good at all. I was near frantic with despair. I had to do something!

I started to run down the tram lines in the oat crop to chase the bloody thing back towards our field, but as soon as she saw me she took off like a train in the opposite direction and now headed toward the aforementioned Newburgh Priory, one of the area's most beautiful parklands and gardens.

"Don't let her get in there," Alan shouted. "She will end up in their gardens and maybe in the lake!"

Oh my! Oh my! Oh bloody Christopher!

I kept going, knowing I had little hope of catching her, but a stroke of luck followed.

Before she reached the carefully manicured gardens of Newburgh Priory, she jumped into a deep dry ditch running around a large wood. And then she disappeared from sight once again!

Several frustrating hours later, now darkness had fallen and there was no sign of her, we gave up for the day to do our remaining work on the farm all the time bewitched, bothered and bewildered that half a tonne of animal, our animal, was roaming loose around the countryside. I didn't sleep much that night, if at all.

I was up and out at 5am in the pickup to renew my search. There are miles of off-road gamekeeper tracks and I was about to become very familiar with them over the coming days.

No sign of her. At the end of one of the tracks is a pair of very large wrought iron gates leading directly onto the main road to the lovely village of Coxwold. They were open. I decided I would close them and hope she would not attempt to get onto the road, cause an accident, even loss of life or end of geraniums in the exquisite gardens of Coxwold.

I drove into the very grand Newburgh Priory itself and held my breath as I looked out across the magnificent lawns leading to the lake. They hold weddings and village cricket matches here throughout the summer. No sign of her, thank goodness. I Imagined the carnage she might cause!

This went on for a week. I had notified the estate's gamekeeper, I'd spoken with Frank Peckitt who has some Limousin cattle in a grass field not too far away. I'd spoken with my good friends Tim and Ann Robson who farm some of the land. Ann was very reassuring!

"Oh, we once had one out for over two weeks," she said.

My fellow farmers were so relaxed about it, advising me that she would, eventually, be found. My nerves were in tatters.

One whole week later, a Sunday morning, Kate

accompanied me on my now daily early morning tour of Newburgh Priory to try and find this bloody animal!

And there she was! Halle-bloody-lujah! It was Kate who spotted her behind the hedge next to the track. What now?

Kate suggested talking to her calmly, but we never had chance! As she saw us, she jumped up and ran off into the adjoining field of wheat! Here we go again!

We drove quickly down the track, as I knew Frank Peckitt's cattle field was next to the wheat field. Could I head her off and force her towards his grass field? It was worth a try. Anything was worth a try!

I decanted from the pickup and ran down the tram lines of the wheat field, but no Beltie appeared. I was exhausted, tired and by now an emotional wreck. I hadn't signed up for this when I had decided to become a cattle farmer!

Kate was trying her best to keep calm and to also calm me down! We got back into the pickup and drove slowly further down the track to see if we could see her.

As we passed Frank's field, Kate shouted, "LOOOOK! She's in the field with Frank's cattle!"

I cannot convey the relief that came over me. She was in a field! A grass field. Okay, not our field, but in a field with other cattle.

She must have spotted Frank's cattle as she had run down the wheat field and must have jumped the hedge to get to them.

It was over. The past week of worry, sleepless nights and going out of my mind was finally over. She was in a field with other cattle and would likely remain there until Frank collected his cattle in the autumn. It wasn't worth doing anything more.

We drove home and had a whisky. It was only 10 in the morning, but deary me we needed it!

I spoke with Frank and he was happy to let her remain there and get bulled by his Limousin bull. We collected her from his farm in the autumn and took her back to our farm where she was reunited with the other three Belties that had remained in our field and had been bulled by Duke.

I got Laura our great vet from Bishopton Vets to come and PD them (which means checking they are pregnant). Even Laura was wary at this task as they were still quite lively, but they were all positive in-calf. Great news.

Now to sell them as soon as I possibly could and get back to normality just with our lovely Whitebreds! No way was I going to risk this utter stress going on any more. I had all four of them in a secure pen in my barn, they were all in really good condition and they were all pregnant.

I found a buyer for all four and he came and collected them. What a load off my mind when they were loaded on his trailer and off they went. I had only got back what I paid for them but that didn't matter. They were gone! Thank heavens!

We still rent the field in question and this year Spring View Henry is there with nine Whitebred bulling heifers. It's a calming place and Kate and I enjoy going there on a summer's evening to check them all.

We often think about that Beltie running wild and loose for a week and the trouble she caused us. But I also spare a thought for her too. She must have been frightened. And as for those wrought iron gates on Newburgh Priory – I still want to close them every day I pass them!

CHAPTER 36

PIGS

Tummy Rubs

I know my pigs. If there is one species of animal that has remained at my heart throughout my life it has been pigs.

Farrowing, like calving and lambing, is a very exciting time. For me, with pigs, it is an incredible and wonderful thing to watch. Just before farrowing the sow starts to make a nest. She starts picking it up.

You know from that reaction that farrowing is imminent, but the real way to know she is going to start farrowing very soon is to squeeze the udder, the nipple, and if there is milk there, there will be piglets born within two or three hours, of that I can always practically be certain.

I love rubbing the udder line of a sow. I'll never grow tired of it. It's one of those special things with a sow. They grunt away so contentedly. I rub their tummies up and down. It's just a lovely thing to see her so settled and happy.

I know you can't be doing that in a commercial situation, but it's fine for me and I will say, 'I'm here, it's me, I'll try and help you.' It's that personal touch and I'm sure the sow enjoys and understands that my touch is there for comfort.

One of the most wonderful things ever is that on the side of the sow's tummy you can see the piglets all moving inside her. I smile about it now while writing these words.

It's incredible. All these new lives.

But that tummy rub. That's still important to me each time.

The actual farrowing bit is incredible too. You can tell when the sow or gilt is starting to farrow because she will be on her side trembling. The milk is there, the birthing fluid. You kind of get to know through experience then how long she should be.

Sometimes she may have one and if there isn't another within half an hour you start thinking of investigating to try and help. That's when you have to put your hand in.

With me being fairly big in the hand and arm department it means I have to sometimes cover my hand and arm in lube and get in as far as I can to feel for a piglet, particularly if it is a gilt and there's one either blocking the way or just not coming out properly.

Often one of the quickest ways to get a piglet out if it is coming headfirst is to get your finger into the mouth of a piglet and slightly down its throat. It sounds a bit gruesome but that is a way. Piglets are born with eight sharp teeth, two each side, top and bottom, and because you've got your finger in there it will bite you.

Kate and I had this one occasion when we had a gilt farrowing. It was around midnight. I knew something was wrong because she was straining away. I'd had a go at trying to get this piglet out but I'd needed Kate's slimmer hand to go in. She could feel this pig, but just couldn't get it. We had both worked on the sow for two hours before we gave way to the inevitable.

It was time to get Julian again!

I remember Julian saying that he was really looking forward to it. That he'd not farrowed a pig for so many years. This piglet that we'd had trouble with was blocking the passageway for the others, because after Julian had got it out the others all came out at roughly five-minute intervals.

If the gilt hadn't had Julian's assistance it would probably have ended up dying of fatigue. It would have just given up pushing. All of its piglets would have died too.

There was nothing so dramatic. Julian came along and within minutes he had the piglet out, followed by a number of other heathy piglets who, despite the traffic jam the first one had caused, didn't seem to have suffered any ill effects at all.

Another success for our good friend.

CHAPTER 37

TAGS

My First On-Screen Role

If there is one good decision we have made whilst we have had Green's it has been to invest in a laser to produce animal identification tags. By law every farm livestock animal has to have an identification number and tag that provides information on where the animal has been from birth to end.

It is the means by which all animals' movements are recorded providing full traceability and stems back to such as foot and mouth disease and BSE and the control of animals relating to notifiable diseases when it was found sometimes difficult to ascertain where diseases may have started.

What these tags do is to enable every animal to be traced back through to its farm of origin and there is then a record of where every animal has been and where it is now. It is vital in ensuring that outbreaks of disease are understood and pinpointing locations, not as a witch hunt but to assist in swift action being taken and in the right places.

Every farmer in the country that keeps livestock has to purchase tags that have individual identification numbers. And as new stock is born, whether they are lambs, calves or piglets, every farmer needs a constant supply of tags.

We wanted to supply something different from the competition, firstly because the other professional ear tag companies that had produced tags had supply issues and secondly because we thought we could offer a better service.

I had researched the market and had come up with a new business idea that we called Lazer Tags. We purchased a machine that lazered the identification numbers on to the tags while farmers waited for them, rather than sometimes waiting a day or two for supplies.

Generally, lots of farmers only realise they have run out of tags at the last minute, or may have realised before that time but not done anything about it because they have been busy on the farm undertaking other more important tasks. Then it comes to lambing or calving time and all of a sudden there is a major panic to get some.

Farmers might think one morning that they will go and tag some sheep. They have probably had that many new lambs born that they want to spend a day getting bang up to date. Then they go to their box where they keep the tags to find they're out of them.

They don't want to wait a few days because they've decided now is the time and that's where we did really well, because with us printing them at Green's they could call in by phone and we'd have their order ready for collection within an hour. It was a massive boon to our business.

We had paid serious money for our Lazer Tags printer that produces the physical tags twenty at a time, every five minutes. Farmers could then come in, no matter how close they were to needing them, wait for them to be printed while they had a tea or coffee, and get back to their farm to attach them to their animals' ears.

It was and still is particularly useful when farmers are taking stock to market and suddenly realise one or two of their stock have lost their tags. Cattle need two tags anyway and they regularly come off just through the hustle and bustle in a shed. This way, rather than not taking their stock to market, where the animal would be rejected, or to a slaughterhouse where the carcase would be binned and losing perhaps £1500 to £2000 worth of beast, they can come along and their stock can be ready to go that day rather than delaying.

I knew this was a great service and thought it would be a great idea to have our own video of what we were doing to show on livestock market TV screens where they show advertisements and also to appear on our website and social media sites.

Chris (Berry) writes these books for me and has also presented many TV shows about farming that have appeared on satellite TV's The Country Channel, making them through his farming magazines *Farming in Yorkshire* and *Farming in the North*. He has also presented video coverage of many agricultural shows such as the Great Yorkshire Show, Ryedale, Driffield, Thornton le Dale and Nidderdale on various channels, YouTube and social media.

It was Chris I turned to in order to produce our 4-minute video presentation. This led to him scripting, editing and directing my first ever on-screen role telling customers all about Lazer Tags. Way before Farmer Chris as a brand was ever invented!

What I remember is it was a bitterly cold, foggy day when we shot on location at Spring View Farm and Chris decided that I should appear with my sheep, at the time Mules, on my hill. I was frozen and kept forgetting my lines. It is the first time I had ever had to use a script. I kept looking at the lines trying to memorise them.

What I can tell you is that I was certainly no 'one-take guy'! I just could not remember the whole of a line. I'd get part of the way through and then an impending sense of doom came over me as I lost confidence that the next words or even the very last word wouldn't come. And it wasn't as though I had anything difficult to remember!

Chris kept reassuring me that it would all be fine, that I would get it in the end. All I had to say was, 'If you've got sheep, you'll need some of these', or something like that. How wrong can someone get it? You'd be surprised how many times!

It was the same with the cattle and probably even worse when with the pigs. I just could not get my head around memorising the words. Chris and his crew were very patient. I think they told me that I wasn't the worst they'd ever had – or maybe that was just me telling myself I couldn't be that bad, surely!

But what came out in the end was something I was actually very proud of, promoting my own new business. But the stars of the show were definitely our customers. Chris had this idea of farmers talking about Lazer Tags and about Green's. They were fantastic, absolute naturals. And they were the people that others in the markets talked about afterwards.

Little did I know at the time, but that was to be only the very first of my on-screen roles that would see me appear on so very many of *The Yorkshire Vet* series and then get the amazing opportunity to appear as one of the mainsprings of a celebrity reality show with a young man who is now very much set to become a household name.

But what I can remember most vividly on that day when we filmed the Lazer Tags video is just how cold it was when you are not moving about on our hill.

The sheep played their part really well too, they certainly knew where the camera was.

CHAPTER 38

PIGS

Barney

One of my favourite boars has been Barney. He's a pedigree registered Oxford Sandy & Black boar who we took on from a farm in Southend. He'd worked on a herd down there and his owner was simply wanting him away to a good home where he could work his magic, as he had done for his herd.

Sows come into heat five days after weaning, but I don't tend to have the boar with the sow until the second time of asking when they come into heat on the 26th day after weaning. It's all just a matter of letting the sow have a little more time. The boar won't bother any sow until a sow comes into heat, but they have a sensory perception of when is right, just like bulls with cows coming into heat two or three days beforehand.

They know, these boys! Maybe we could learn a thing or two about this kind of thing! It might save a few relationships along the way!

There are only four male bloodlines that are registered with the Oxford Sandy & Black breed and they are Alexander, Alistair, Clarence & Jack. Barney was a Clarence bloodline.

Barney didn't cost me a lot of money and worked on my sows for a couple of years before we gave him to another breeder near Thirsk. That's the way it goes if you're a boar. You are a journeyman with a different piggie harem every few years. It's the other end of the male farm animal life. If you're born a tup, bull or boar you're either on borrowed time immediately or you're on to a good thing.

A boar's, tup's or bull's extended life is probably the equivalent of a porn star. They are there to perform!

Oxford Sandy & Blacks are regarded as a medium-to long-size pig breed with an ideal temperament, and Barney was true to form. He was such a good-natured, nice boar to work with that you could do almost anything with him.

Which was just as well because, like any Oxford Sandy & Black boar, he had grown tusks that I have always felt it is safer they are removed, for the boar itself because of how they grow and to avoid being gashed by them when working closely.

What happens is the tusks start growing when the boar is about 2 years old. They grow on the bottom jaw and they stick up. The problem is they rub on the outside of the boar's cheek and I became concerned for him as much as myself handling him.

Barney's were starting to curl around and looked to me as though they were getting quite big and going into his skin and I imagined they were becoming uncomfortable for him.

I'm not certain but I would imagine that tusks were grown and were used for either fighting or at least defending the rest of the herd years ago, but these days they serve very little purpose and most breeders will remove them to avoid any chance of being injured by the tusks. One false move and you could receive a serious if unintended gash to your ankle or arm, or worse, if you are in the wrong place at the time.

I decided that it would be best to remove Barney's tusks exactly for these reasons.

The ways in which you take them off can vary. The

usual manner is by using cheese wire, but I've also heard of junior hacksaws being used.

I invited Julian back on to the farm to help me with the task the first time I'd had to undertake it and had thought it might make another interesting piece for *The Yorkshire Vet*. I was also happier that I had someone else to show me how to do it the first time around. I've done it on my own ever since.

Although Barney was a reasonably chilled out boar we were taking no chances and gave him a sedative called Stresnil, which makes the boar drowsy. That's when our trouble started.

The fact that we had doped him made him very cross and so we tried another dosage, but because of his size he was resistant to the doping at first and kept fighting back. I hoped that the very reason I was doing this wasn't about to put me in danger of Barney's tusks, the very reason for what this exercise was about. This was a boar weighing in at 400 kilos. If he went bananas it could have been carnage.

After we had doped him the first time the plan had been to do the deed. Julian had made the first injection and we had got the cheese wire ready to go up to him.

I'd said to Julian something along the lines of, 'You think you are just going to walk up to this boar and open his mouth?' That's when I realised that Julian is a much smarter man than I am.

He said, 'Oh no, that's your job. You're the one who is going to be opening its mouth while I get the cheese wire.'

I have to tell you that the next scene was like something out of a Laurel & Hardy movie with me thinking what another fine mess I'm in here. Picture the scene. We have a drowsy pig wondering what's happening. We have two men creeping warily through the straw. Almost like one of those old children's games where if Barney opened his eyes you would have to stand stock-still.

When Julian told me my role, I said, 'I don't think this is going to work.'

Wasn't Barney going to react, even though he was drowsy, as soon as we opened his mouth? Correction. As soon as I opened his mouth?

Sure enough, as soon as we'd got to him he shot up, grunting and complaining. It wasn't like Barney's normally mild-mannered way, but this wasn't a normal Barney! Somebody had given him something that meant he was angry.

That's why Julian administered a second dosage – and it was also why we gave up on the idea of conducting this in the open.

We got him into the cattle crush in the end and held him in the crate so that he couldn't move.

I put a rope around his top jaw and held it up and Julian leaped into action. I was surprised how quick the whole operation was. Once you start using the cheese wire on the tusk it comes off really quickly because the tusks are hollow.

Since then I've de-tusked on my own, given the experience I had with Julian, and it was a really gentle boar who I didn't dope at all. I put him into a cage that I take out on the back of my tractor sometimes and dealt with him while he was in there. I'd wondered whether he would just let me do it and had thought that maybe if I didn't dope him and just took his tusks off without any drama it might work – and it did!

Going back to Barney, he looked as though he felt so much better after de-tusking. As for Julian and I, the bit where we were moving slowly towards him after the first dosage all seems a bit to me like a scene from a yet-to-be-made *Carry On Tusking*!

CHAPTER 39

PIGS

The Corkscrew

I always find people are fascinated by pigs. In the past few years my TV appearances have led to interest in my social media platforms and the pictures that generate most response are invariably those of my Oxford Sandy & Blacks.

While they are the most photogenic and cutest of breeds they are also one of the most docile, friendly pig breeds you could ever wish for and they never disappoint in the way they are.

I keep ours in the best possible environment. They're outside until late autumn/early winter, where they would always prefer to be and where they come from originally as they are not just known as the plum pudding pig because of their colouring but also the Oxford Forest pig because, like a lot of pigs, they started out in woodland.

During winter they are inside, which helps the soil and lets the grass return after having been destroyed from their natural tendency to root, but they are not kept on slats when they are inside. I muck them and provide fresh straw every day.

When visitors come to our little farm, as some started to last year, they are drawn to the piglets, these wonderful little coloured piggies that are sucking into their mums, the sows. It's such a lovely sight that it gets that 'ahhh factor' every time.

What I'm trying to do when we have our Open Farm

weekends starting this year is to have at least one sow having just farrowed so that people get to see this joyous time.

One of the things I'm able to tell people when they do visit at that time is that every piglet has its own teat that it sticks with from its mum, which is decided as soon as it is born. It develops a pecking order among the varying size of piglet.

The front teats produce more milk than the back teats so you will generally find that the bigger piglets will be those on the front teats and the smallest, the runt, will be on the back teat. Pig litters differ in number and size. You can find your sow farrows anything from one – as I was very embarrassed about – to 14–16.

Generally, the Oxford Sandy & Black will farrow something between 8–14 piglets. Usually inside three days the piglets have normally doubled their size and those on the richer and greater amount of milk will grow more quickly than those down at the other end!

There is also usually much fascination, especially if a sow is on heat at the time we have visitors, in the boar's penis!

You see this long thin thing that extends quite quickly and when it is extended, usually to around a foot and a half long, it has a corkscrew to its end. It is a left-hand thread by the way, don't ask me why, it just is! And the thread locks into the cervix of the sow. Some ladies wince at this point when they are told, because they are thinking about a corkscrew that you use to take a cork out of a bottle, but it is really very natural.

The cervix is tightly closed to prevent infection in the womb and the thread provides the insertion point required for the boar to ejaculate and impregnate the sow.

In all of the years I worked on intensive, commercial sow breeding units, serving the sows was the most critical time of the week, when you might have as many as 500 sows on site and so there was always serving every week of the year. It's far different for me now with just five sows farrowing two litters each per year.

Back then, the serving of the sows was the most critical point of the week because without getting the sow pregnant we had nothing and so I was trained to help the boar serve the sow.

We have not shown this or any other type of exercise involved with pig reproduction on *Celebs on the Farm* on Channel 5 or MTV, but Julian and I were involved in what became one of *The Yorkshire Vet*'s best TV moments of all time a few years ago. Let's just say we didn't handle the situation brilliantly on first go, that led to the camera crew and producer doubled up in raucous laughter!

When I was working on large-scale sow units you had to stay with the sow until the boar had mounted the sow correctly. That's because often the boar didn't know which orifice he should put his penis in and that led to a slight dereliction of duty, which is no good to man nor beast!

I had to help and guide the boar's penis into the vulva and wait until you knew he was locked on. Remember the left-hand thread at this point into the cervix. The sow is stood rigid at this point as the boar, now excited, is chomping away with froth known as pheromones coming out of his mouth, stimulating the sow.

When the boar's penis is locked on you can put your hand on his bottom and when you can feel his rectum pumping in and out he is ejaculating into the cervix and he will be there between three to four minutes until the job is complete. That's what serving is all about – and it is the boar's whole purpose.

It's not a bad life at all! I hope it doesn't give you trauma next time you open a bottle of wine and start thinking of threads!

CHAPTER 40

COWS

Bertha

Aah, Bertha! Just hearing her name brings back lovely memories. Some hairy ones as well, but mostly good things.

Bertha was one of the first pedigree Whitebred Shorthorns we bought and my goodness she was a real character. She was a proper little madam, but the most beautiful cow and I loved her to bits. She was quite fat without being overfat, but with a great behind to her. What you might call in human terms great childbearing hips.

The problem with Bertha was when she had just calved you couldn't go near her. Woe betide you if you tried because she would have you. We learned that much very quickly. She was such a protective mother. She never actually got me, but she would come at me.

She was already an older cow when we got her, but she served us really well. She had produced a lovely bull calf for us on her first calving since coming over from Helen Chard's herd in Lancashire and had gone on to produce heifer and bull calves.

One particular year I had to take more extreme action when she had calved and we needed to look after the calf because of the conditions it had been born in – and Bertha was certainly not playing ball.

This particular day she had gone into what we call

'calving corner', which is where the cows go to when they calve outside. It had now got to that point in her calving when it was too late to get her inside but the problem was I could see for miles that this awful thunderstorm was coming.

Bertha started calving during the storm, when it felt like hell was unleashing all its fury. Thunder, lightning, rain lashing down in torrents. What a bloody job we had.

Bertha calved in all that. She had no problem calving and gave birth to another beautiful calf, but we wanted to get it inside and out of all this dreadful weather to give it the best chance as the point of the storm passed over.

We had no chance! Bertha was typical birthing Bertha, an absolute madam. There was no way she was going to let anyone near and we just had to let her and her calf get absolutely wet through. All respect to her mothering nature for being protective, but there was a point where something had to be done and this was it.

I put the cage I use for isolating stock on to the back of my tractor. It's big enough to get a calf in. I backed up to 'calving corner', managed to waylay Bertha with a bucket of food while I got through all the wet and mud and quickly got her calf into the cage, jumped back on the tractor and set off back to the shed. Bertha followed. We did it! Mother and calf safe!

I hope Bertha appreciated my efforts.

I had another hairy time with her when I took Bertha and her calf to Ryedale Show, which you may have read in an earlier chapter.

In the autumn of 2018, when she had been with us for 3 years, I noticed this problem with Bertha's eye. It was red and swollen and I just thought she may have got some kind of seed in it, causing the swelling and redness, but she wouldn't let me get hold of her to see what was wrong.

I thought I'd better get Julian to come and have a look

and I never forget the day he came. *The Yorkshire Vet* camera crew had arrived about an hour before him and had been talking about getting some opening shots, the kind of stuff they use to add to the filming.

I remember clear as day saying that I didn't know whether it would be worth filming this at all as I thought we were only talking about a hayseed.

The best way Julian had of examining Bertha was to get her into the crush to avoid her moving. And then the day took a downward spiral when he pulled her eyelid open.

Julian said, 'Chris, you need to have a look at this. It's not very nice at all, and I think it's cancer.'

I looked and there was all this growth on the lower eyelid. It was all red and horrible.

Julian then told me there was not really anything he could do with it, apart from to leave it and manage it, so that she didn't get any fly problems.

Bertha was in-calf and that was the reason for not doing anything there and then. It was better that she had her calf first. That's what happened. We kept managing Bertha's eye by putting whatever we could on it to help.

Julian kept coming to see Bertha, checking on how she was progressing, but the eye was getting no better.

In Summer 2019 while her new calf was still sucking her, Julian told me my options for Bertha were two things I could do that would sort out the situation. He said that I could have her culled or he could take her eye out!

Take her bloody eye out?!

It wasn't an angry response from me, more shock than anything else, but Julian said he could do it, and it had to be the eye because the cancerous growth was in such a way he couldn't just cut the growth out. He said the whole eye would have to come out and he would have to stitch up where the eye would have been, stitching top to bottom.

I thought such a lot of Bertha. She really was very special to me and with such a strong emotional connection I was torn. I thought what this would be like for her to go through – and me!

And there was another thought that flashed through my mind. There was no other cow registered as pedigree to my knowledge that had the Berscar prefix. But the biggest motivation I had was simply this. I wanted to keep her – and so we made the decision for Julian to take out her eye.

It was 19 August 2019 when Julian had said to have the crush ready to put her in outside. He said he'd bring someone with him as it was a two-person job and of course *The Yorkshire Vet* TV crew were here too. This really was a first. Taking the eye out of a cow.

It was a beautiful summer's day. I had Bertha in the crush and my heart was pounding.

I'm thinking that this is the only way we can save her, but then that I'm responsible for taking an eye out of this beautiful animal. I'd not signed up for this when I'd been thinking about having my own farm, but you have to deal with anything and everything with animals. Livestock farming can be very hard and very stressful, but then it can be the most rewarding thing too – and I don't mean money-wise!

Julian's would-be assistant hadn't materialised. He'd come on his own. 'Don't worry,' he'd said, 'we can do this between us.' US!?

He asked me to set up a table to put all of his instruments out. I magicked up a table from a sheet of plywood and a couple of barrels and he put a big cloth upon it. We had an al fresco operating theatre, right there!

The operation began. I was holding Bertha and talking to her trying to keep her calm. Julian used two bottles of anaesthetic in and around her eye and I've never seen anything like it. It was very hard to watch. It was the most awful, gory, bloody thing you could ever see and I was feeling so sorry for Bertha.

There was blood running out of her head to the bucket below, but Bertha just stood there. Didn't flinch. She can't have felt anything because of the anaesthetic.

It took Julian about 40 minutes. He took out her eye and the growth and more and had Bertha all stitched up. I now had a one-eyed cow, but at least he'd got rid of the cancer, or so we hoped. Off she trotted out of the crush and back into the field within minutes. She didn't seem to have any problems at all and she was probably more concerned about getting to her calf, who duly started sucking back on her immediately.

After a week or so I became really worried again. Where Bertha's eye had been was now so swollen it was as though there was a golf ball underneath her stitches. Julian came back but said it was normal and it was the cavity filling up with fluid. It would all be reabsorbed, part of the healing process, and with no infection. I'd thought he might have to release the fluids, but no, that was the worst thing that we could do. Let it heal properly.

It healed perfectly. The hair grew back over it. Just wonderful. I thought, we've done this. I've a cow with one eye but she's not in pain, normal, in good condition and she was back in-calf. There's no stopping our Bertha. Job done.

It was a year or so later, maybe more, that I noticed that she'd started to get a swelling where her eye had been. It would swell and then pop with pus and heal up again. Maybe it was okay?

No, she started to get worse and then she started to lose condition. This beautiful, always well-fleshed, lovely fat cow was losing it.

I really started to worry. With all that had happened

she had never lost condition. She'd always been healthy. She'd had Beatrice sucking on her when she'd had the eye taken out. She'd had Christopher the year later in 2020 and she'd had Tommy in spring 2021.

It had been while Bertha was in-calf with him that she began struggling and it was as though she knew it was nearing the end as she was really struggling by the time she had Tommy. I could not recognise her from this beautiful, big cow that she had been and I really think she gave everything she had left to produce Tommy and once she had calved him she had nothing left to give.

It was a hard decision to make because she was the cow we'd had at the start and that I really loved, but I also told Kate that I couldn't bear seeing Bertha get any worse.

Fortunately, our neighbour, Cooper Wilson the licensed slaughterman, came when I contacted him. I brought my lovely old cow in from the field for the last time. My poor old girl who was going to skin and bone and who I think knew all that was going on because she was a little reticent to get in the crush, but you got the feeling didn't have the strength to complain.

Cooper's really good with animals of all kinds and just said: 'You're alright 'owd lass.' He did the deed and she just dropped and that was it. Bertha my beautiful first Whitebred Shorthorn cow was gone.

Livestock farming really can be so heart-breaking and my heart was broken that day. But that is also part and parcel of what livestock farmers have to deal with every day.

I have great memories. Kate and I shared some fabulous moments having Bertha with us, and you know what, all of those remain. What a grand old girl.

Now, just excuse me for a moment while I sort myself out, won't you.

CHAPTER 41

LESSONS

*Flies, Blood Spurting Sheep & Another Idea
That Didn't Work*

I hold my hands up. I have made some massive mistakes in my life. And I've made one or two since we've been here, as you've probably now read, but there are sometimes things that you don't make a mistake over, you just learn, and often through bitter experience.

We now have more land than when we started. We rent about 30 acres in addition to the 10 acres we bought. The idea of having more land is to be able to have more grazing opportunities for the sheep and cattle. When it is put that way it all sounds so easy, but it's not quite that way because you suddenly find that there is something new thrown at you that you hadn't expected.

A field is not the same as another field. It might look that way but it may be quite different to another. Just ask any arable farmer and they will tell you the soil quality differs often throughout the field and within a couple of yards. Where the field faces affects how things grow, hedges affect habitat, whether it is flat land or on a hill, changes the field's dynamic. I hadn't appreciated all of this until I put some of my sheep on to some of this new land we had acquired.

Now the problem could have been the sheep, it could have been the field and it could have been the weather.

All I know is that we put some sheep on this land and I

have never seen the amount of flies that descended on my sheep. It wasn't blowfly, it was some kind of head fly. I had never seen anything like it in my life.

It was in the summer of this particular year when the weather had been a varied mixture of mild, wet and hot. Even though they had been clipped and had fly spray on them they were covered in these swarms of flies, hundreds around each head. The sheep kept escaping. I'm sure I would. It must have been sending them around the twist.

We had quite a job catching them all and I quicky decided that this field obviously wasn't suitable for them. We shifted those that hadn't already escaped back to a field that they knew.

That was another reason why we also made the decision against going for a lot of sheep. We decided that we wanted to keep them on the land we own, where we could see them and also which isn't too bad for flies and certainly nothing like the plague of the horrible things we had that summer.

Flies are a constant threat to livestock. We've had three cases where we've had mastitis in cows because flies get into the udder and spread disease. If a cow gets mastitis it then does not produce any milk from that quarter and so it can be a massive problem.

The plague of flies was an instance of learning about our farm, our land, what it offers and what we have to watch out for. Farming teaches you new lessons every single day and that was one of them. Fields.

There are times when things go wrong that really aren't my fault and one of those happened to one of our Kerry Hills. It was another one of those 'I've never seen anything like it in my life' moments.

We had a shearer in to clip our sheep and the most awful thing happened. The shearer cut into the milk vein, which is a big vein that runs down the ewe's tummy. Oh my God! It was a fountain of blood!

I was shocked. It was the most horrifying sight, seeing the blood spurting out, but the shearer was exceptionally calm. He stemmed the flow and just said that I'd better call the vet otherwise she would bleed to death.

We were with Skeldale Vets at the time. It was a Sunday. There was no song and dance about it. Within five minutes of being here the lady vet had the ewe stitched up and it was absolutely fine. Another lesson. Don't panic!

Although I didn't ask, I had the feeling this kind of thing happened during shearing from time to time. Certainly, the shearer and the vet both took the whole episode in their stride.

But this next story brings me back to a recurring theme of this book about having not thought things through. It's another field story, but this time with my cows.

I had this wonderful idea of keeping some of my Whitebred Shorthorn heifers out for this last winter on a piece of land we rent. My reasoning was that it is nice dry land and the breed is naturally hardy and would prefer to be out given the choice rather than inside. It's better for their health too.

The thing is where I had put them was a dry field, but I'd not thought of what it would be like to get to them with silage, their feed. And the fields I had to go through to get to them were not dry, in fact they were distinctly wet and puddly.

To get to my heifers with the silage involved driving my tractor with the feed, through three gates and over two fields. You should see the ruts I made and the unintended damage done to my fields and particularly to the areas around the gates where I constantly had to jump out of the tractor, open the gate, jump back in, go through the gate, and then jump back down to close it again before the sheep made a hasty exit from one field to another.

The practicalities of doing this I hadn't thought through at all, but then this had been my first time trying it and now I knew. That's why some farmers that have been on a farm all their lives can look at you as some kind of dimwit. They probably learned all this when they were twelve.

I decided on bringing them back home in the shed where I had the space for them. It had been a good intention but hadn't worked.

That really is farming for you. You are always learning.

CHAPTER 42

THIS YEAR – 2022

Calving

Springtime is the most glorious time of year on the farm. It's the time when new life is all around us. Well, it should be, but it can also be the most harrowing time.

It's a time when all you have dreamed about, your plans for your stock, can move forward with the new lives and how you intend to grow your flock or your herd dependent on what is born.

It's also a time of anxiety over whether it all goes well for your animals and frustration when it doesn't.

Livestock farming is always tinged with sadness as well as euphoria. When a new lamb or new calf is born it is the latter, but when we lose any animal at birth, whether a lamb or ewe or both, or calf or cow or both, there really is emotion.

I don't think all of the general public really realise this fully. Farmers, in the main, love and care for all their animals and from time to time you lose stock. It's not because you've done anything wrong. It is nature taking its course.

But of course, it is also your business. If you've invested, as we have, in quality stock you need to see a return and losing animals can alter your plans considerably.

As this book was being finished in order for it to be published in time for the book launch at our Open Farm Weekend in June we were in the throes of both calving and lambing.

Calving was over halfway through and it was looking good. We'd had a few earlier disappointments way before calving when we had Tabitha, Elizabeth and Heather having problems, but that had still left us 14 to calve, as Elizabeth is now due to calve in August. I just couldn't calve 13! That's asking for trouble.

It's girls that I really want, heifers, for all of the reasons I've talked about and after eleven calves born we had five heifer calves and six bull calves.

The girls are: Primrose born out of Katrine Cassi; Bertha out of Beatrice, Beatrice having been our dear old Bertha's daughter; Dolly out of Snowfall; Symphony out of Snuffles; and Lady out of Creeside Queenie.

The boys are: Sebastian out of Ben Ledi Hannah, so named after a famous song by one of my favourite groups ever, Steve Harley & Cockney Rebel; Apollo out of Katrine Holly; Zeus out of Parton Penelope 18; Hector out of Parton Penelope 16; Titan out of Royal Heather 2nd; and Oscar out of Creeside Twinkle.

I had a bit of a panic over Holly before she calved because in the couple of days before calving her teats had been dripping with milk and I was beginning to think something was wrong as I'd not seen that before. Her bag was so full.

When I rang Bishopton Vets I was reasonably calm and said that there was no need for a visit. I just wanted to speak to a vet for a bit of advice. They have a number of vets at the practice and they're all great. This time it was a guy called Jack who listened to me and then said:

'Chris, there's nothing wrong with that. She's fine.'

With those words of reassurance I rested easier than I had for the previous two nights when I went to bed.

One of the most helpful pieces of equipment we have installed recently is CCTV. We now have three cameras in the livestock shed that we set up ourselves. We can move them about for whatever we want to watch and at this time of year we have two trained on the cows and one on the ewes.

The cameras have helped enormously as in past years we have been getting up every other hour in the middle of the night to walk down to the barn to see what's going on. Now we have the cameras linked up to our iPhones and we can look every time we want during the night without having to do the trek unnecessarily.

What a massive difference it has made to our wellbeing.

The next morning, after having spoken to Jack, I looked at my iPhone around 6 o'clock and there was Holly lying on her side.

I immediately knew she was calving. I got up, went down and she had this beautiful bull calf, absolutely stunning. I helped her to pull it out in the end, but there were no problems, no drama, everything was as it should be – and Jack had been absolutely right.

We made a massive change in our feeding regime of the cows this year. We decided that instead of feeding them a lot of silage in mid-pregnancy, which they love, we would feed them hay, which is a bit boring and bland, but they do eat it.

One thing I love seeing is my cows eating silage, but unfortunately what happens is they get too fat and that leads to complications with calving because the unborn calf gets too big.

It seems to have worked. My cows have looked a lot leaner for calving and every cow and heifer has calved beautifully.

The other two cows that are now not due to calve this year – Tabitha and Heather – are still with us for next year. Tabitha had problems getting in-calf. She wouldn't hold, but as she is one of Bertha's daughters we particularly want to keep her. She's only a young cow and so we've given her six months off and will try her again for next year.

Heather is an old cow, her full name is Barlaes Royal Heather, and has good bloodlines which is why we are keen to give her another chance. We bought her from Donald, so there is an emotional attachment there too as well as her breeding.

Our stock bulls are now Ben Ledi Duke and our own homebred Springview Henry. I'd had high hopes of him doing well at Carlisle in autumn but we have since decided that he has a job to do here.

We now have a herd of around 25 cows and heifers to be bulled this year. I have a feeling that around the 20-mark is the size that works best for our farm, but bearing in mind that some may not hold in-calf from the 25 we could end up with around 22. If we end up with all 25 in-calf we may sell two or three of the in-calf heifers.

We will be splitting the herd in two for this year's bulling. Springview Henry had already served two out of three females he had been running with in March and will be with nine bulling heifers in one herd; and Ben Ledi Duke will bull all of the cows that he's not related to.

Henry told me he was very much looking forward to getting started on the heifers when he was to be put with them from April 1.

We were also very much looking forward to taking Springview Joseph, one of our young bulls, to exhibit on the Whitebred Shorthorn Society stand at Beef Expo in May after having been asked to do so.

And we are planning to take Springview Joseph to three agricultural shows this summer at Ryedale Show, Thornton-le-Dale Show and Cleveland County Show.

We may even also let Joseph and Romeo have their first times with some of the ladies this year.

Exciting times indeed!

CHAPTER 43

THIS YEAR – 2022

Lambing Nightmares

Without doubt the rare breed part of our story is very important, as has been the journey that has led us to the Border Leicester breed.

I thought I'd cracked it when I saw the prices being paid, that I paid, at Carlisle and from reputable breeders elsewhere, to buy quality ewes, but this first year's lambing, that we were near the end of as we finished this book, has been an absolute nightmare!

Now don't get me wrong here, we all know that a ewe's only ambition is to die, but someone somewhere has been pulling my chain this year! I know that a certain not very nice thing is said to just happen, but I am not kidding, we have had everything. It is as though someone has taken exception to us having these bloody things!

Even before we reached lambing we'd had a ewe that died, one that went lame and back to its previous owner and two that were barren – but that was nothing compared to what then happened as lambing was about to get under way.

One decided to abort, just a week before it was due to lamb!

I can feel some older or just more experienced sheep farmers giving a wry smile. They've probably heard it all before, but I was devastated at 4 o'clock that morning when I found these two beautiful but dead little lambs up on the hill. I know I keep saying this. I just could not believe it!

And even that's not all!

If you read the earlier (Ch. 26) I'd gone to Carlisle to try and buy replacements for the two barren ewes and the one that riggwelted and died. I'd bought one in-lamb ewe, which was due a single lamb, and two ewe lambs to go to the tup this year. And what has happened?

The two ewe lambs have got Sheep Scab! These bloody sheep have brought Sheep Scab on to my little farm. So, now we have infection!

I just found out they'd got it as we were getting to the end of lambing. I'd noticed these two ewe lambs were fractious. They'd been biting and rubbing themselves ever since coming back from Carlisle. We hadn't had an instance at all on the farm before. Their skin had become red raw.

It's not their fault, obviously, the poor things.

They could have picked it up at the livestock market or they could have already had it before they got there. Everybody who puts sheep into a market has to make sure their stock is treated for Sheep Scab before they take them as it is highly infectious and debilitating, but I can fully understand that it may have happened just beforehand or it may not have even been through the owners of these sheep as they may have picked it up from others. Who knows? All I know is s*** happens, and here it was happening to me, yet another calamity.

Sheep Scab is started by mites and then transmitted between sheep, so this could now go through my whole flock! The flock I have spent serious money on since last year.

I've had to engage a shearer to come and clip all of the wool off these sheep and two others they were with. We've had to get the vet in again, to inject them all. Money,

money, money.

Oh, and to add even further woe, we've had a deformed lamb too, a ewe lamb, that had to be put down because it was such an unfortunate mess. We've had two more like that too, that died from the ewe that had quads. They have been showing classic signs of having the virus Schmallenberg, which brings about deformity! Again, Oh my!

So, here's this year's score from my breeding ewes. One dead, one sent back to its original owner, two barren, one that aborted, one that had a deformed lamb, and another that had two deformed lambs. That's six pretty useless ewes, as one of them, Quadie, had two that are alive as well as the two dead ones. Plus infection on the farm.

And as if that wasn't enough, even our lambing split of tup lambs and ewe lambs is way out of whack – not just from what I'd hoped, but also the natural order of these things.

My hope had been to be able to attend Carlisle next year and sell maybe six to a dozen ewe lambs for the kind of money I'd seen pedigree Border Leicesters go for, and the price I'd paid, earlier this year. We haven't a reputation yet, but even allowing for ours going for a little less perhaps because of this I was still confident of a good return. It's not the same market for pedigree tup lambs, although the better ones do go for decent money and so it was the ewe lambs I wanted.

Up to the point of writing this we'd had 14 live, fit lambs this year. And what had we had? You'd anticipate a 50/50 split or somewhere near wouldn't you?

Oh no, not me, not us, not these bloody Border Leicesters! We've got four! Four girls! Out of 14! That's a 28 per cent hit rate of my beautiful ewes, and let's not forget this because they are still fabulous to look at, producing tup lambs. Only four girls! It would be laughable if I wasn't so upset.

So much for my masterplan of taking all these ewe lambs to Carlisle. It's almost hardly worth the effort for four!

And, in addition to all of this, these bloody lambs I've had born have suffered from entropion eyelids! This is when the lower eyelid is inverted and the eyelashes rub on the eyeball and cause irritation, which then needs treatment with antibiotics.

It's not at all pleasant and not nice to treat as sometimes you have to inject antibiotics into the lower eyelid. We've had a third of the lambs suffer from it and apparently it is hereditary, most likely coming from the tup, which then should not be used for breeding! Oh my! Talk about problems with these sheep!

But you know, at the end of the day you've got to be resilient. You're looking after animals and it's still a pleasure to have them. The thing to remember is that it isn't everything that is going wrong. There are still lots of wonderful things happening.

Bringing them in for lambing has brought us closer to them. When they were out on the hill they were quite wild at times, but inside they have become very friendly. We can almost treat them as pets now. They will allow us to stroke their heads and talk to them.

Kate has been bottle-feeding a ewe's triplets, feeding them several times a day, and they're all looking good.

It's not all bad, and we've already decided that we are going to try and show two of our shearlings at this year's Great Yorkshire Show.

Now that could really be an amazing experience!

CHAPTER 44

THE YORKSHIRE VET

Julian

Firstly, a really big thank you to Julian – *The Yorkshire Vet* – not just for the times we have spent together but also for writing the foreword to this book and this next chapter.

Our TV incident with Elsie when we inseminated her will live long in many viewers' memories, but here's Julian to tell a few of our tales in his own words.

When Chris first contacted the practice having just moved on to his farm I was the first to visit. Our relationship started off low key, but everything got a bit more interesting when the telly arrived at the practice.

Chris was naturally very good in front of the camera, explaining about his animals and very passionate about his farm. From a telly point of view it is that passion and enthusiasm that the programme-makers really like and Chris had that in abundance. His personality and love of his rare breed animals lent itself really well to the programme.

It was a good marriage of expertise and exuberance and we got on really well as I loved his enthusiasm for his farm and animals. He also helped me out. Chris would ring, say what problem he had and if I was coming would I like to come and film whatever it was for the telly. It was really helpful because not all farmers are as open as that.

Chris was always happy to share his stories with the wider world and we struck up a quite interesting and sometimes quite comedic relationship.

I'd been on the farm the odd time or two, a calf with pneumonia, a TB test and I had seen some of his pigs from time-to-time, but Elsie was something different from the routine. I think Chris had anticipated this might have some comedic potential, so when he asked for help in inseminating Elsie I agreed.

The idea was that he needed another pair of hands. Chris had obviously been quite experienced at this in his earlier career and my experience of inseminating pigs went back to when I was a student vet on a pig farm just outside of Leeds where there was a huge herd. I would spend all day inseminating sows.

The comedy started when I arrived and Chris had this package delivered in a massive envelope by the postman and it had to be signed for. It had come from Northern Ireland. The postman asked what was inside. Chris's answer made him smile.

We opened the envelope, capturing it all on camera, and there's this bottle of semen, all the tackle and the instructions, which all seemed quite funny. Then we set about inseminating Elsie.

I was a bit rusty and it turned out Chris was a bit rusty too. Add one agitated sow and you had a perfect mix for something to go wrong or at least turn into a telly moment. I don't know whether Elsie had been inseminated before but she wasn't really amenable.

One of the ways of telling when a sow is ready to be mated is to sit on her back. If she stands still it is all systems go, that's the main sign.

There's Chris sat on Elsie's back trying to tell whether the sow is ready to be served, and it was borderline. She kept running around. Whether she sensed Chris wasn't a pig, whether she didn't like him or he was too heavy, she took time to settle.

It ended up a happy outcome for everyone because she was pregnant, but it was also comedy gold so far as the production team was concerned, what I'd call a little bit of a Last of the Summer Wine moment with Chris sat on Elsie and me screwing in the catheter and then snapping off the top of the bottle of semen to great hilarity!

It made for excellent telly. The viewers liked it. The production team liked it and Chris got the bug I suppose, because any time he had anything vaguely interesting it was a case of come and look. It was nice. He was very happy to share his farm, his animals and his experiences with a wider public and willing farmers are always good news when you're making telly programmes.

The relationship between a farmer and a vet can be quite a personal one. The farmer is often looking for someone to help when things don't go to plan, maybe in the middle of the night and when you are genuinely tired, stressed and worried, but our relationship grew into more than that.

Because Chris and I had worked quite closely, not just on the farm but on the camera on the farm it sort of exposes you a bit more. Ours became not just a farmer and vet relationship but one that included 1.5 to 2 million viewers.

And we had some really interesting storylines.

Bertha's story of her eye was a much more serious telly moment.

Bertha was one of Chris's first cows and he had quite a fondness for her. She had developed this problem of discharge from her eye which hadn't responded to treatment and Chris had called me to take a closer look.

I was immediately worried. It didn't look right, quite abnormal. It wasn't a case of conjunctivitis and it made me instantly suspicious that it might be a type of cancer that cattle can get on their eyelids and the structures around the eye. It's not common but where it appears is on the white faces of cattle.

I treated it fairly conservatively at first with some injections. It got marginally better, but not enough for me to become any more confident that my first impression had been right. I started to broach the subject that it might require surgical intervention and that Chris might even need to have Bertha put down.

The tumour was on her eyelid and just cutting that off would have left her in a perilous and painful condition. In cases such as Bertha's what you need to do is take out the eye and all of the structures around it completely. If you don't the cancer just comes back again.

Chris was understandably quite anxious about the surgery and I was cautious over explaining how successful the surgery might be. It would be a big procedure, there are a lot of blood vessels around and it was not something to jump into without full consideration.

Bertha was in-calf and plenty of farmers would have said to let her have her calf and then send her off to the knacker man and probably not even bother at all in trying to treat her during her time in-calf, but Chris was keen to do what he could for her. She had her calf before surgery in the end.

On the day we were all anxious, including the camera crew. Chris made up a kind of surgical table for my equipment and we began the al fresco surgery. It is always exciting operating in the open.

You don't undertake this kind surgery under full anaesthetic, you do it under a local anaesthetic and that meant numbing quite a sensitive area of the body. Bertha was a bit headstrong and restless, but she calmed under the anaesthetic.

It was pretty gruesome surgery and 10 minutes in I think Chris was probably wondering whether this was what he'd expected and was probably also extremely *worried about the outcome as there was so much blood, and work required. He didn't exactly go green and pass out, but I could tell he was fairly traumatised.*

But it went well. All of the cancer was out and she was back able to live a normal happy life. She had her calf and went on to have more. It had been a nasty problem with a nice solution. A really happy story that I'm sure the viewers loved.

To me it showed Chris's commitment to animals, to Bertha, to his Whitebred Shorthorn cows and to the breed.

There was Donald the boar too. Chris said he'd been named after Donald Trump, because he had a gilt called Ivana! Donald needed his feet trimming and his tusks cutting off as Chris said he was getting quite worried because Donald was throwing his weight around.

He was quite a handful. I'd turned up following afternoon surgery and we sedated Donald. My idea had been to jump into the pen and wire off his tusks, but every time I went towards him with Chris he got up and started running around. Chris was telling me to be careful, that Donald was dangerous.

We topped him up with even more sedative and eventually he was totally flat out. I wired the tusks off, rendering him safe for Chris and everyone else, but bizarrely he then totally lost his libido!

Ivana never got inseminated by Donald. Now there's a news story! Since then I've always been wary of trimming tusks!

Chris and I have had some good times, some late nights and early mornings of stress and anxiety, but it has always been a really good relationship and friendship.

Thank you so much, Julian!

CHAPTER 45

OUR FARM

The Future

By the time you read this our lives could have changed massively again and hopefully for the better. We have so many plans for our little farm and Kate and I are looking forward to devoting ourselves wholly to Spring View Farm and Spring View Rare Breeds.

We will already have completed the first of our new ideas by the time you are reading this book as we will have held our first ever Open Farm Weekend, which was to be held on the weekend of Open Farm Sunday which was due to be held on farms throughout the country again on June 12, 2022.

We had been hoping to host or own Open Farm event in both 2020 and 2021, but we were scuppered like everyone else with pandemic restrictions, but this year we were determined to host it and, just like me, I decided that one day wasn't going to be enough. Ours was to be run over two days!

They are called LEAF Open Farm Sundays because the organisation Linking the Environment & Farming is behind the initiative that offers the general public, through each participatory farm, the chance to be hosted by farmers and their families who explain more about how they run their farms, about food and farming and the methods they adopt for sustainability.

This is very much where my Farmer Chris brand comes

in. Last year we had 200 visitors and FC fans booked to come, but had to cancel due to the fears everyone still had about Covid even though some restrictions were easing.

This kind of event is where Farmer Chris will be in his element!

It's something I see us doing more of, not just on the annual Open Farm Sunday but several times during a year. I'm not sure how many yet, but it's what I want to be able to do. It's about giving something back, telling people more about food and farming and using my little celebrity status mixed with my little farm to give people a good time looking at our animals and learning more.

One thing is for sure and that is we will be looking forward to welcoming everyone, whether they are local people who just want to see what we've done or those from further afield who are interested in animals, farming or just meeting Farmer Chris, that's FC by the way!

When we have open days I will be trying to make sure that we have some sows that have just farrowed. I hope to God I don't strike unlucky and have another litter of one! Now that would be embarrassing! 'Hi everyone, I'm Farmer Chris, and here's how many piglets our sows have!' It doesn't bear thinking about.

We will always have a number of Whitebred Shorthorn calves around and Border Leicester lambs. And some will know a good friend of ours who has also appeared regularly on *The Yorkshire Vet* – Jackie Barlow, who will be bringing her alpacas.

I am very keen on our rare breed status and see part of our role being to champion the Rare Breeds Survival Trust. I see us becoming more closely involved with the organisation. We've just launched our own Spring View Rare Breeds website.

We all know how much people like to get into the countryside and how much they enjoy TV programmes about farming and rural areas.

One of my other plans is for us to create some kind of farm visitor centre within a new building that we've just altered for the purpose. We don't want to go down the line of being open all the time, just certain times perhaps in a week and then special Open Farm Days during the year, maybe as themed days such as for lambing time.

I am also looking forward to working a little more with LEAF and the Rare Breeds Survival Trust (RBST) on education visits for schoolchildren as part of my farm visitor centre idea. Prearranged visits, rather like the Open Farm visits, where everyone is booked in advance of the days.

I'm particularly keen on getting the message across about where food comes from and why rare breeds have reached rare breed status – and how those who visit can help by consuming more of the meat that is produced by these breeds. It's so important. We haven't to be afraid of telling people of all ages that this pig will go on to make pork pies, bacon, sausages or ham. Of course, it needs to be done with care and sensitivity, but it still needs to be said.

We were or are (whenever you are reading this) delighted to be hosting our first ever Whitebred Shorthorn Society Open Day in September 2022, which is for farmers and cattle breeders, either other Whitebred breeders or those from other breeds.

Our herd, if not the biggest pedigree Whitebred herd in the country, is on its way to becoming so and we have Donald Hendry and Helen Chard to thank for that, as well as Richard Greenwood our neighbour, he of the Kramer machine!

Without Helen having her Whitebreds at the Great Yorkshire Show in 2015 we may not have come across the breed; without Donald I wouldn't have had anything like the number of cattle we have today; and without Richard being eagle-eyed I would not have been at York livestock market to buy Ben Ledi Duke!

Spring View is now a respected name in the Whitebred world and that's why we were asked to exhibit at Beef Expo 2022, host the Society Open Day 2022 and why I've been asked to become a Whitebred judge. I feel humbled every time I am asked to do something for this wonderful, beautiful breed.

It is truly an honour and a privilege but at the end of the day I just love my cows. They all have their own personalities and at the moment Snuffles is definitely one of my favourites. I can go up to her, put my arm around her neck and rub her head.

And there is of course another side to having cattle and one that is vital if rare breeds are to increase in number – and that is the connection between food and farming.

Did you see the *Hairy Bikers* on their latest tour of the north? They stopped off at all these farms and at one of them they tasted Whitebred Shorthorn beef!

I know how good it tastes, but we haven't got into selling it yet as we have concentrated on building up the herd, keeping and selling females and selling bulls to other breeders, but we've got to that stage where our herd is so big now that we are always going to have a surplus of bulls.

What that all means is that we can be more selective over which bulls and bull calves we keep in future and we've started that this year by selecting three that we think will not make our grade breed-wise and they will become our first Whitebred Shorthorn beef. Maybe the Hairy Bikers will come back for more?

Tommy Banks, the Michelin star chef who has the award-winning Black Swan at Oldstead, already buys our Oxford Sandy & Blacks, so perhaps Tommy will be interested in our rare breed beef too.

We've had a rough start with our Border Leicesters but we are going to persevere. We've only been in them for less than a year and so we need to give them a chance. I'd like to have a couple of Valais Blacknose too, and I still like the idea of having Hebrideans again, but we really need to give these Border Leicesters a fair shot.

I would love to be talking about hosting our own Border Leicester Open Day in future, once we've got the flock truly settled.

The most important thing of all in our so far relatively short time at Spring View is to remember how we came to be here.

Without Kate and I having Green's at Thirsk none of this would have been possible. Green's has given us so much. Firstly, our togetherness, our marriage. It has taken us to faraway islands; be a racehorse owner for a while; and come here.

We grew the business, I then took my eye off the ball for a while, but ever since being sat in that accountancy office in Leeds where we were offered £1 for our business we have fought back and fought long and hard.

We could have been out of business, out of this farm and I might never have become Farmer Chris.

We had two options. Lie down, get rolled over, go bankrupt and let people take what they wanted and we would just walk away – or we could look hard at our business and set it back right. We both had more guts, more fight, more courage and more inspiration than to let it go. And our inspiration was this place, our little farm.

We made hard decisions, the hardest part being having to make people who we really liked redundant, but we completely realigned our business, reduced our trading, but made our company far more profitable. We'd got too big for our own good.

Green's became a highly profitable business and has remained so, which led to an approach to buy our business once again in 2021 and by the time you read this book we may no longer have Green's at all.

I will be the proudest man in the world if that happens, because we will be debt free and with money in the bank.

I am so looking forward to welcoming visitors, FC fans, animal lovers, schoolchildren, anyone who wants to know more about food, farming, livestock.

I know our little farm isn't big, but it's ours and it's a lovely place with a beautiful view and beautiful animals. I just can't wait to share all of that with everyone who comes!

CHAPTER 46

FARMER CHRIS

Television

I never ever thought I would be appearing on television let alone being turned into a minor celebrity as Farmer Chris.

It has only happened through having the farm, the rare breeds, having Julian as our vet. It has all progressed from there.

I loved it straight away. I've always been the kind of person who likes to be in the forefront. If I was able to sing I would have loved to have been able to stand on a stage and entertain people.

Kate says I do entertain people, that you've only to look in our store when I'm talking to people, that I have that way with me.

When Julian turned up one day with a film crew we just got on famously.

We were with Skeldale Vets, the practice that Julian and Peter were both a part of when *The Yorkshire Vet* started on telly, as our dogs were registered with them.

Julian had been on the farm for the first time in spring 2016. Something to do with pneumonia in a cow or calf. But the next time he had the crew with him. I think they were trying me out on camera and probably liked the location. It is beautiful.

We bounced off each other. There was a rapport. Julian then said that if I ever had anything that might look good on telly to let them know.

They came back within a month to film something to do with the pigs. They liked the plum pudding pigs. I don't think they used what they had filmed. That's when I came up with the idea of AI-ing Elsie.

It was all good fun. I felt I was able to get a little exposure about our rare breeds and what we were trying to do – and I was also living for the moment and enjoying working with Julian who is a great vet, lovely person and now a good friend.

I liked that there were people around with cameras and headphones. There was no money in it for me, it was just a nicety. I never thought about being a TV star. It was nice to have contributed and I also knew a lot of my customers would watch.

I couldn't believe how many people came into my country store and said 'I saw you on telly' and they still do because of the repeats. Then you get all the wags. 'Think you're a bloody farmer now do you lad?' and 'No wonder we never see you in the shop.' It was all typically good humoured. 'You'll know a bit about what farming's really like now, won't you lad?'

It actually worked out really well for us because now people saw Kate and me differently because they now knew we had a farm of our own. In one way it was mildly frustrating because both Kate and I have been involved in farming all of our lives in some way. And I already knew what it was like to be a farmer. I'd worked on everything from intensive pig units to extensive sheep farms.

But in another way they were right, as it turned out. I really didn't quite know what having my own farm was like. I hadn't thought it through, of course, but I've learned so much in the past seven years. And there's a lot more to learn.

And it's great when I get people come up and say 'Aren't you Farmer Chris from the telly? I follow you on social media.' One of the most amazing things was being sent a message from Adelaide in Australia that said, 'G'day FC. Just seen you on TV. You were great.' The shows go right around the world.

I was stunned when I received the call to try out for *Celebs on the Farm*. I've been fortunate enough to have been Farmer Chris, the judge, for three series. Who would have thought that? A lad from Wigginton!

I've no idea whether there will be a fourth series, or whether I will be on *The Yorkshire Vet* again, but the experiences I've had and the lovely people I have met has been one fantastic ride. I wrote about the first two series in my first book, which is still available, *Farming, Celebs & Plum Pudding Pigs – The Making of Farmer Chris* and then in autumn 2020 we filmed the third series of *Celebs on the Farm* and for the first time in North Yorkshire!

We were at Ash Tyson's Stepney Hill Farm on the edge of Scarborough and due to Covid restrictions the whole production team, cast, crew were all located at the same hotel in Scarborough. It was the first time I'd stayed in the same overnight location as the others and while that's not how the producers really like it, because they want me to be a bit aloof from the rest as they don't want me going soft on anyone, it was nice being around everybody.

Ash, his wife Nicola, all their family including his dad John, were absolutely spot on and loved the whole experience, just like me. It was great to be in North Yorkshire for the filming. I'd loved being on the south coast for the first two series but this was getting closer to being in my own backyard and Ash and Nicola were fabulous hosts.

If ever you're thinking of going to Scarborough for a holiday they have some fantastic holiday accommodation now with a holiday cottage that has a hot tub with it and a shepherd's hut. It is such a lovely location and I know the camera crew loved it especially.

The lovely Kerry Katona won the third series, which ran on MTV in February 2021, and she was such a really nice young lady. She has had to cope with so much in her life. I have such respect for Kerry. She's a very determined girl.

I felt a real bond with her over the way she has had life throw things at her, as my life has sometimes done, but shove a farmer's cap on her and she was very much the part.

When I first met Cheryl Hole I didn't have a clue who she/he was. I'd never seen *RuPaul's Drag Race* TV show. When I first met Luke, dressed up in all the spangly costume I wondered what the producers had given me! Goodness knows where he puts his bits when he dresses up. I really have no idea, but he turned into one of the best celebrities we have ever had on the show.

Luke put everything he had into every part of the programme and was so close to winning. It just shows that you should never judge on first impressions. And he is also a fabulous young man too.

Chris (Berry) asked me to name the celebs from the first two series that have probably left the most lasting impression on me, so here goes:

Caprice – I'm still kind of shellshocked that Caprice keeps in touch. She's world-famous. I'm not. We got off to a bad start on screen when I gave her a bollocking because I felt at first that her attitude wasn't right, but this gorgeous lady, whose poster had adorned my son's bedroom wall in his teenage years, came around full circle and became a very good friend. I was amazed by her determination to win, which she very nearly did.

David Potts – I will never forget the first day he walked into the barn. He had lippy on, make-up all over the place, eye shadow and bronzed bare legs, mincing about. I remember thinking 'Oh my!' But in two days he's abandoned the make-up, there was no messing about, he got stuck in and looked just like a farmer with his flat cap on. You can't not like David. He is such a lovely, friendly, funny young man – and the boat incident with Arg (James Argent), who was certainly not the best contestant we've ever had, is in my humble opinion one of the funniest telly moments ever!

Chrissy Rock – We had this almost on-screen romance when I look back at the series now. Chrissy was very passionate about the animals and was in tears many a time when things weren't going the right way. I feel that Chrissy cares so much about everything and everyone. I really like Chrissy very much, such a nice lady.

Charlie and Hayley – I think of these two together because they are both lovely kids. Charlie Edwards won the WBC Flyweight title as a boxer and Hayley Hughes was on *Love Island*. Her strong Liverpudlian accent and blonde hair sometimes give the wrong impression of Hayley because she's a cute kid who knows exactly what she's doing with marketing, clothing and perfume, and when she was shepherding the others should have listened to her because she was exactly right.

Charlie has achieved amazing things in his young life and I just love the promo pic of us both squaring up to each other when he had his world championship belt on. I know how much Charlie loved being on *Celebs on the Farm*, probably more than anyone else I've seen. He even asked whether he could come back to watch the others after he was eliminated. Nobody else has ever done that. He drove back himself the next day. A true sportsman and a fine young gentleman.

And while I'm mentioning sports people I have to give a special mention to Kadeena Cox and Paul Merson. What Kadeena has achieved on the track in athletics and cycling with four Olympic gold medals, two at Rio and two in Tokyo, is phenomenal. Kadeena's now making a name for herself as a TV presenter and she was lovely to work alongside.

Paul is of course a footballing legend and I will always be so proud of how he overcame his fear of animals in taking part in *Celebs on the Farm*. A really nice, all-round, good guy.

Some of those who have taken part in the series have not bought into the whole farming experience as much as others, but that's life! Most have given it a good go, one or two have looked as though they would rather be somewhere else, but everyone has been good to meet and get to know.

But the bright star that has shone throughout all three series has to be my mate and the show's presenter Stephen Bailey who, as this book goes to print, is finally getting the recognition he deserves, appearing regularly on the BBC. He's been on nearly everything recently from *Pointless* to *Richard Osman's House of Games*, he's selling out on his stand-up tour and he's even recorded his own BBC Radio 4 stand-up comedy special.

Stephen came up to the farm for lunch last summer (2021) when he was playing a gig in Ripon and was on top form. I've seen his live act twice now, in Newcastle and London and he is very funny and a great performer. I've met his boyfriend Richard who is a really nice guy too.

Stephen and I have a great relationship on the show and it would be brilliant if we ever got a fourth series.

Filming *Celebs on the Farm* and *The Yorkshire Vet* has been one of the happiest times of my life – and here's another!

When I received a call from *The Yorkshire Vet* production team at Daisybeck Studios about filming a Christmas Special and playing a role in a scene they were re-enacting from Charles Dickens's *The Christmas Carol*

I nearly fell off my chair.

It was Olivia who rang and said they would like me to come along and film a scene with Peter Davison.

Peter Davison?! Bloody 'ell!

Now I was in dreamland! I watched every episode of *All Creatures Great & Small* when it was on television the first time around and Tristan, played by Peter, was one of my forever heroes.

You what?! Play alongside Tristan? You bet! We even named one of our bulls Tristan.

I was to play the Ghost of Christmas Present. The filming was at Ripley Castle in this massive old bedroom. Peter is in the bed as Scrooge. He remembered every word, every line, every facial expression, every take – and it would probably have only taken one take if I'd got my lines right! But there am I, playing a part that is going out on national television. Three million people tuned in for that one programme! I don't think they tuned in for me, but I have to tell you it has been the highlight of my TV life!

The Yorkshire Vet Christmas special, three series of *Celebs on the Farm*, meeting heroes like Peter Davison, international names like Caprice, outstanding sports stars like Paul Merson, Charlie Edwards and Kadeena Cox, music legends like Duncan James, Kerry Katona and even Tony Christie when Kate and I were invited to be guests at a literary event when his book was launched; becoming friends with Julian and Stephen. It's all been the most fantastic ride.

But the most important person of all, without whom none of this would ever have happened, is my lovely wife Kate who supports me in everything I do – and the most important decision we ever made together was buying Spring View, our little farm.

I hope you have enjoyed the tales from my little farm. Come and see us soon!

EPILOGUE

I have been lucky enough in my life to have travelled far and wide. It started with a trip to Libya in North Africa way back in 1965. My Aunt Ellen was a nurse stationed out there and I flew out on my own at the age of 7 to stay with her!

I was also lucky enough to go skiing in Austria with my school at the age of 14. Since then, I have been to many amazing parts of the world on holidays and adventures.

The Maldives hold a special place in my heart as it is where I proposed to Kate and where we later returned on honeymoon. Kate and I also took a 4-night trip to the gambling capital of the world, Las Vegas, as my youngest son David decided to get married in the Bellagio Hotel in this incredible city.

While we were there, we took a helicopter trip over Lake Mead, the Hoover Dam and landed in the Grand Canyon and drank champagne before flying back over 'The Strip' in the dark.

Mauritius was another beautiful destination in the Indian Ocean where I fished for marlin, among other things!

The beautiful Balearics are also a favourite and I have been many times to Majorca, Ibiza and Menorca. Turkey and Malta are destinations that also bring back many wonderful memories.

The Republic of Ireland is also a favourite, where we visited the last port of call of the Titanic, Cobh in County Cork, which was then called Queenstown. We drove around the Ring of Kerry.

Northern Ireland, especially the road trip up the North Antrim Coast from Larne to Ballycastle.

In more recent times, Kate and I have visited Scotland, starting with a 5-night cruise visiting Orkney, the Western Isles and Ullapool. Since then, we have explored the Outer Hebrides by car, travelling up to Oban and across the Irish Sea to Castlebay on the wonderful Isle of Barra.

One of our favourite trips was to the St Kilda archipelago which is the most remote part of the British Isles, 40 miles out in the Atlantic, west of the Outer Hebrides. Next stop – America! A truly incredible journey and an experience we will never forget.

But the best and most satisfying journey of all has been to Spring View Farm, nestled within the Howardian Hills in an Area of Outstanding Natural Beauty.

It has taken blood, sweat and tears to get here.

Kate and I started on this, our most satisfying journey, in February 2004 when we started in business together. We lived in a rented cottage in the lovely village of Crayke back then, but as the business grew we were able to buy a cottage in Husthwaite where we stayed for seven years before the dream was achieved in November 2015 and we got the keys to our little farm.

Now, nearly seven years later, after building up the farm and continuing our daily work at Green's Country Store we are close to selling the business so that we can become 'proper farmers'!

This is a double-edged sword in a way because we both know we will miss the buzz of being in business and meeting our loyal customers every day. But it will give us financial security and as we are both approaching 65 it will give us more quality time on the farm. We hope!

We are also looking forward to having the time to show some of our animals. As you've read already, we have been asked by the Whitebred Shorthorn Society to represent the breed at Beef Expo, held at the new Darlington Mart, in May 2022. The Rare Breeds Survival Trust have also asked us to take two Whitebred heifers to the Great Yorkshire Show in July 2022 and we have selected Katrina and Peggy.

It has taken us seven years, but now we have an established herd of Whitebred Shorthorn cattle, a fledgling flock of Border Leicester sheep and a herd of Oxford Sandy and Black pigs, plus Kate's horse Lorna, our four Jack Russells and the chickens.

We now farm 40 acres and are about to start our farm visitor centres so that people can come and visit us and meet our animals too. We are hoping to work with LEAF (Linking the Environment and Farming) to bring parties of schoolchildren to the farm as we want to help the future generation understand the importance of farming and where their food comes from.

The future is bright. The future is Spring View Farm Rare Breeds!

See you all very soon, I hope.

Farmer Chris

FARMER CHRIS'S
FARMING FACTS

Some interesting facts about farming in the UK!

1. Farmland covers about 64% of the UK with more than 20 million hectares of land – that's the equivalent of 30 million football pitches.

2. There are around 192,000 farms in the UK. Only 20% of these are over 250 acres. The larger farms cover three quarters of the farmland. Around 50% of all holdings are under 50 acres, with many farms being family-run units. Soil type, topography, and climate determine the type of enterprise that is suitable for a particular farm.

3. The average age of the British farmer is 60.

4. Agriculture employs 476,000 people, representing 1.5% of the workforce, down more than 32% since 1996.

5. East Anglia produces enough barley to make 2.5 million pints of beer each year!

6. The UK produces 7.8 million tonnes of wheat for bread-making annually and the average person buys 43 loaves per year.

7. 5.5 million tonnes of potatoes are produced in the UK each year. That's enough to make around 27.5 billion packets of crisps!

8. 60% of food eaten in the UK is grown in Britain and 77% of shoppers agree it is important to support

British farmers.

9. The iconic British countryside that farmers manage generates over £21 billion in tourism income each year.

10. A large tractor can do in one day what used to take 100 people a week!

11. Did you know that if you put all the UK's hedges together, they would circle the earth 20 times!

12. There are 10 million cows in Britain and each day they produce 60 million pints of milk. That's enough to fill over 15 Olympic swimming pools. Cows are also much cleverer than you might think – each one can recognise its own name.

13. Pigs are far from 'boaring', in fact they are considered the fourth most intelligent animal (after chimpanzees, dolphins, and elephants). They are also sprinters, reaching speeds of 11mph and their squeal can be as loud as 115 decibels, 3 decibels higher than the sound of a supersonic airliner!

14. There are over 35 million sheep and lambs in the UK – we produce more sheep than any other country in Europe. But did you know that sheep can recognise up to 20 different human faces, and they prefer a smiling face to an unhappy one!

15. Farming is a big part of the British economy and it's so important that everyone supports Britain's farmers, especially in these very turbulent times. Please, wherever possible, buy British and do your bit to keep this vital industry going.

16. Remember – No farmers – no food!

Farming, Celebs and Plum Pudding Pigs!

The Making of
FARMER CHRIS

by **Chris Jeffery**
with **Chris Berry**

Chris Jeffery (TV's celebrity judge on *Celebs on the Farm* and regularly-featured farmer on *The Yorkshire Vet*) here tells his remarkable life story, from farmer's son to pig farmer, to milkman, insurance adviser, meat humper, animal nutrition representative and farm supply shop owner, before television beckoned at sixty years of age and 'Farmer Chris' was born.

Chris's amazing journey has taken him from a village near York and a now distant world of Shire horses, girls, rugby and his close circle of pals, to a life map that includes Suffolk, Northern Ireland, a Russian love affair, owning a racehorse and proposing to his third wife in the Indian Ocean. Today he is back with his first true love – animals – running a rare breeds farm with his beloved pedigree Whitebred Shorthorn herd and his plum pudding pigs.

Follow Chris's highs and lows as he (sometimes) lurches from crisis to crisis, but always comes out smiling.

Farmer

Chris

GREAT NORTHERN

www.gnbooks.co.uk